AF427975

Table of Contents

Page No.

Preamble

The study of literature can be approached from several angles. It can be examined from linguistic, historical, sociological, psychological, and autobiographical angles. Furthermore, it can be examined via the lenses of psychoanalysis, deconstruction, post-modernism, structuralism, lesbian feminism, narratology, marxism, new historicism, cultural materialism, postcolonial criticism, and stylistics. These viewpoints can be broadly categorized into two main categories: linguistic and thematic. However, let me provide a warning at this point. Form and content, method and matter, and style and subject are not mutually exclusive.

The current work aims to illustrate how stylistics might be applied to literary analysis. Stylistics analyzes literary works using linguistics' techniques and discoveries. It provides concrete evidence to back up feelings on literary works. It makes recommendations for fresh readings of literary works based on linguistic data. It explains the process of creating meaning in literature. When it comes to understanding and appreciating literature, stylistics is crucial.

This work, which is an exercise in stylistic study of Vikram Seth, will be very beneficial to Seth enthusiasts as well as educators, scholars, and students of Indian English literature in general. The author has carefully noted, divided, and talked about a few distinctive aspects of Vikram Seth's aesthetic.

An in-depth analysis of Indian English novels and Seth's role in them opens the book. After doing so, the author discusses the nature of stylistics, its application to the study of literary works, and its breadth. The author then continues by going over the main ideas found in Seth's books. The book's fourth and fifth chapters provide insight into the salient features and stylistic motifs of Seth. The final chapter expands on the topic of deviations and foregrounded lexical and grammatical patterns that define Vikram Seth's style.

Dr. Subodh Kumar Ray

PREFACE

The tradition of Indian writing in English is relatively short but qualitatively it is not considered second to writing in native languages. Indian English Literature is one of the most authentic voices of India which expresses Indian ethos. It has now moved away from the earlier Indian English literature both in style and in the treatment of its themes. Among the galaxy of Indian writers in English (indeed there are too many and it would be practically impossible to mention them all), Vikram Seth has carved a niche for himself by his versatility and creative experimentation. Initially, he wrote in a self-imposed exile in America and China, and then his homeland, recently England and Europe were his working grounds. Like many English- knowing upper class Indians, he uses English besides his mother-tongue. Like many Indian creative writers in English, he has adopted the alien language for his creative expression.

However, it should be mentioned here that several English writers of the post-1980s, either live outside the subcontinent or have spent considerable years abroad as part of the Diaspora migrancy. As these writers are deracinated from their roots, they tend to explore their past in their creative writing. And so, the contemporary Indian writing in English is prominently characterized by such diasporic writing., the writers of Indian Diaspora, like Salman Rushdie, Vikram Seth, Rohinton Mistry etc. are highly reckoned for their subject matter as well as forms.

Seth plays a crucial role for the development of Indian English literature, not only as a novelist but also as a poet biographer, memoires and travelogue writer. He ornamented his novels by using different styles like sonnet, verse, epic and music. Vikram Seth has been acclaimed as an international writer and his works are some of the most daring innovations and experiments with form in Indian Writing in English. Vikram Seth is not only one of the fascinating and multitalented writers but one of the most important and prominent diasporic writers of post modernism also. He illustrates different social realism and multicultural aspects. Seth always uses his classical style in his writing. His style of writing outpaces him from other literatures of his contemporaries. Seth's works remind us of the earlier realists and naturalists in their particular treatment of realism. Seth's use of language, the selection of different geographical locales, his styles of versification and musicality, the inculcation of Indian values in his characters irrespective of their geographical affiliations, and realistic narration in *The Golden Gate (1986), A Suitable Boy (1993),* and *An Equal Music (1999)* capture the readers' attention and interest.

In all his novels, Seth deals with varied themes which primarily form the universe of Seth's fiction. Seth's pre-occupations are varied: loneliness, changing times, corruption, modern thoughts with lack of moral values, nuclear insanity and disarmament, etc. Seth seems to be interested in fulfilled love that leads to marriage and family. In other words, he is just not interested in superficial or romantic love filled with passion but rational love. Each of his novels is based on social stability, security, togetherness and social order.

The book is an attempt to explore Seth's writing style, uses of figures of speech, the narrative techniques of fiction and themes and plot through his novels *The Golden Gate, A Suitable Boy* and *An Equal Music.*

In order to broaden and appreciate the innovative use of language in literary discourse, I hope that the book will be beneficial to researchers and students.

This book is divided into five chapters. In the first chapter, *Introduction*, an attempt has been made to trace the contribution of Vikram Seth in the Indian English literature and fictional world. It also attempts to examine Seth's writing style of novel, use of language and use of narrative techniques. The life and works of Vikram Seth are perceptively discussed.

The second chapter titled, *The Golden Gate: - The Beginning of Narrative Technique*, discusses the thematic concerns of the novel. The novel is entirely about American ethos and it portrays the forming and breaking up of personal relationship, romantic love, life, profession, friendship, alienation, death, birth, heterosexual and homosexual affairs, loneliness, disappointment in family and so on.

The third chapter titled, '*A Suitable Boy: - A Study of Themes and Techniques*', details the issues of national politics, land reforms, academic affairs, inter and intra family relations. The study focuses on external and internal chaos in the families. Seth has done admirable work in presenting authentic characters, convincing situations permeating the rich network of the novel through suitable language suiting different mindsets and condition.

Moreover, Seth is conscious of giving suitable sensibility to the particular novel and all in all he has proved himself as a great genius and presented himself as an ideal for the young rising talents.

The fourth chapter is titled, '***An Equal Music: - A Study of Musical Techniques, An Equal Music***', is set on contemporary Europe. The study focuses on the lives of classical musicians, the emotional and psychological crisis they undergo and finally how they achieve emotional stability.

The fifth chapter, ***Conclusion***, briefly summarizes the arguments and solutions offered by the author in the novels. The study is to analyze Vikram Seth's attempt to show how the characters in his novels endeavor to mount reflections of harmony and offer better solutions for their psychological and emotional upliftment.

Darbhanga   ***Dr. Subodh Kumar Ray***

]ACKNOWLEDGEMENTS

I must first express my gratitude to **Dr P. N. Jha,** (Retd.) Professor, Department of English, C.M College, Darbhanga, for his guidance, cooperation and inspiration to write this book. Despite his hectic life schedule, he has always provided me time and the support needed for this work. I have no words to express my gratitude to for his scholarly inputs, valuable suggestions, encouragement and affection. I am immensely grateful to my Ph.D supervisor **Dr. Akhileshwar Kumar Singh**, Associate Professor, University Department of English, L. N. Mithila University, Darbhanga for his unending encouragement and guidance.

I express my heartfelt thanks to **Dr. Krishna Nand Mishra** and **Dr. Yugeshwar Sah** for their unconditional support, academic guidance, valuable suggestions, and moral motivation.

Last but not least, I am deeply indebted to my friend **Dr. Amarjit Yadav,** my mother **Smt. Indu Devi,** my father **Sri Indrajeet Ray,** my better half **Mrs. Nandani**

Kumari, my son **Amartya Div**, my daughter **Manvi Kumari**, all other family members for their unconditional love, care, and support. I apologize for the acknowledgement if not duly made, and if inadvertently written anything. Hope I will achieve the goal with the grace of God.

Dr. Subodh Kumar Ray

Dedication

*I would like to dedicate this
book to my wife and parents.
They instilled in me a desire
to learn and made sacrifices
so that I may have access to
high quality education from
an early age. Also this is
dedicated to my close friends
who have always supported
me throughout my years of
study.*

Introduction

1. (A) Vikram Seth's Brief Acquaintance

Indian English Literature has attracted a widespread interest both in India and abroad. And it can't be ignored that it's a reality now. It should come as no surprise that a new crop of post independent writers, emerging from a relatively small but sad period of two hundred years of British colonialism, has shrugged off their hang over and arrived on the global literary scene. They have shown the western publishing world that Indian writing can sell. These bold new writers have made daring experiments with fictional techniques. In Indian English fictional world Vikram Seth is one of the leading writers of English fiction. Seth can legitimately claim his place among those Indian English writers who have by their training and background, confident command of the medium, the ability to bend, break and manipulate it in fresh and creative ways. He is a brilliant writer who deserves to be taken seriously, both by the general readers and the discerning scholar and researcher. Seth as an

Indian writer in his poetry and fiction puts emphasis on love and relationships and explores many dimensions in a shifting and changing and corroding background. His creative achievement could be considered as one of the finest in the post 1980's Indian English literature.

Vikram Seth was born in June 20, 1952 in Calcutta (at present Kolkata). His father Premnath Seth was an executive of <u>Bata Shoe Company</u>. His mother Leila Seth was well trained in law in London and subsequently became the first female high court judge in India. She also became chief justice of a state high court, at Shimla. Seth has a younger brother, <u>Shantum</u> and a sister <u>Aradhana</u> a film maker, who married an Austrian diplomat. Seth's family played an important role in his life so Seth has said:

"My father was not a very literary person,

But my mother used to write poetry when she was young,

There were always lots of books lying around,

So, I suppose I was partly inspired by her

Nevertheless despite my father's lack of interest in the art,

It was he who encouraged me to write." (1)

Seth received his primary education in Dehradun, in Doon school. In this school many of India's rich and famous personalities have been taught. This elitist boarding school education equipped Seth with the confidence and the linguistic tools to fit in abroad and it also cultivated in him a predilection for the literary culture of England. In an interview with Pavan K. Verma Seth says "we are all accidents of history we must accept that if you have been taught to play the Sarangi, you cannot suddenly switch to sitar so perhaps, I must accept that English is my lot". (2) He later went to Tombridge School in Kent, England. From where he won another scholarship to oxford to read English, however he soon changed to philosophy, economics and politics from Corpus Christi College, Oxford. He completed his graduation in 1975 from Oxford University. Then for post graduation degree, Seth left for Stan ford University California, U.S.A. It was that being an avid reader of poetry as well, he stumbled upon the translated works of T' Ang dynasty Chinese poet

Wang wei Seth was so affected by these poems that he decided to learn mandarin Chinese Language so that he could read the Chinese masters in the original, and demonstrated his intellectual brilliance by learning the language quickly that he was writing poetry in Mandarin language. By now he had also started writing poetry in English more seriously.

In Stand ford University Seth spent eleven years working on his doctoral thesis. Along with this he did poetic studies as a Wallace stinger fellow in creative writing. He worked with the poet Timothy Steele. Steele's traditionally structured verse with formal rhyme and meter inspired Seth to adopt a similar formal discipline in his own poetry, Seth was also considerably influenced by Donald Davie, the English poet and critic at Stand ford at that time. Both Steele and Davie are fine, format poets and under joint influence, Seth's natural inclination to write in rhyme and meter bore fruit. His first collection of poems, **Mappings,** came out in 1980. After he rejoined the Economics department facing rejection by every publisher he tried, Seth typeset, published and distributed himself, pedaling it around the Bay area book stores and friends, exhorting them to sell if they could and to give them away if they could.

Vikram Seth lived in London for many years and he now maintained residences near Salisbury, England where he is a participant in local literary and cultural events. He bought and renovated the house of Anglician poet George Herbert in 1996 and in Delhi also he owns a house where his parents and he live while on visit to India and maintaine his extensive library and papers. A glance at his poetic collections is attempted here. According to Australian magazine 'Good Weekend', he studies several languages including Welsh, German, French, Mandarin, Urdu and Hindi. He plays Indian flute and cello and sings German lieder especially Schubert. Seth is not only a novelist but also a great poet.

Literature of Indian Diaspora constitutes a major study of the literature and other cultural text of Indian Diaspora. For this concept it's applying a theoretical framework based on trauma, sorrow, specters, identity, travel, translation and recognition this anthology uses the term migrant identity to refer to any ethnic enclave in a nation-state that defines itself, consciously or unconsciously as a group of displacement. Vikram Seth also applies different cultural realism in his works. Like in his three Chinese poets he discoveries Chinese culture, in *The Golden Gate* he talks about American culture whereas in *Mappings* and *An Equal Music,* he written about British culture and in *A Suitable Boy* he describes Indian culture. Through his fictional world he is recognized as an emigrant writer and a person of universe.

1. (B) Acquaintance of Seth's Works

Though Seth is more famous as a novelist but he began his literary career with poetry. *Mappings* is introspective as poet's first collection. It was written while Seth was a student in London and California. In this work, he explores all the themes that recur in his later poetry: The intimate subject matter of love, loss, friendship, loneliness, expatriation, sexuality, relationships within the family, nature and social conscientiousness – all his trademark mock humorous stance. He also touches on public issues as the injustice of poverty.

Mappings introduces us to Seth the polyglot with poems translated from Hindi, Urdu, German and Chinese. Through this first volume Seth served something of an apprenticeship while revealing an early preoccupation with European and Chinese cultural production that has become more pronounced in his more recent work. As in the case of a large number of the nineteenth century poets, Seth draws largely upon an international variety. If romantic ideals sustain the spirit of the nineteenth century Indian poet in English constituting a significant part of their intellectual and creative Milieu, Eliot's prevalence in their poetry lead to a desire for closer approximation of certain international techniques of expression in versification. Belonging to the second or third phase of post modernization in Indian poetry in English, Seth's beginning as a poet is not of a sporadic nature and his power to be able to continue to write verse speaks of vital annexations of the experiences of the past as available in works of art together with techniques of expression. Most of the poems in this first collection were in rhyming couplets, triplets, octave and sonnets.

Vikram Seth has expressed his migrant feeling of loss and displacement in his works. Seth introduced himself to the world as a writer through his first poetic collection *Mappings*. Seth's Diasporic identity and its features are highlighted throughout the collection. The themes of alienation, exile, rootlessness, loss, nostalgia and other experiences of the poet are expressed in many poems. As a migrant writer he has infused his work with the application and experiences of multi- culturalism, hybridity and search for identity. The autobiographical elements play a significant role in the Diasporic writing.

Seth's another collection of poems is known as "The Humble Administrator's" Golden comprises 33 poems in three divisions "Wiltong", "Neem" and "Live Oak" the names of three different trees denoting Vikram Seth's differing connections in China, India and America. They also indicate the poet's keen sensitiveness and intimacy with nature, which form an important structural element, in the poems here and in the earlier volumes too. They also continue the poet's habit of writing in rhymes, half-rhymes or in prose pattern and with wide-ranging references invariably with strong personal point of view.

The next poetic collection is titled *"All You Who Sleep Tonight"*. And it has five subsections a total of 53 poems, including 20 poems of four lines each entitled 'Quatrains'. The subsections are 1. "Romantic Reside". 2. "In Other voices". 3. "In Other Places". 4. "Meditation of Heart". The structural trends are similar to what is given earlier in the previous poems related to love and relationship to nature and to a sense of distress and pain and death at one level and happiness, playfulness, and sense of relation on the other. At the same time there is strong social awareness along with the mind's capacity to be reflective about situations, and to accept distress etc as a part of living.

Seth's next poetic work "From Heaven Lake" was published in 1983. It is a travel book for which Seth won "Thomas Cook Award for the best travel writing". In this travelogue, Seth describes about his travels through Sinkiang and Tibet is popular and compelling autobiographical tale of authors' journey from Nepal to India and many and varied people he meets on the way, though his adventures are both exotic and idiosyncratic. Seth's writing is in keeping with the already mentioned traits of his style: a clear passionately descriptive prose with attention to detail and ability to maintain the reader's attention which later formed the basis of his fictional prose style. Seth's prose as found in his travel book reveals itself to be an adequate means of expressions not only for a book of travel but also for the purpose of novelistic description. Seth observes closely the impact of Chinese communism on what was once a theocracy. Throughout the book Seth plays the role of a wanderer, constructing an Indian Diasporic Persona for himself.

He published his next collection of poems **"Beatly tells Here and There"** in 1992. It is divided into four volumes, a delightful collection of fables retold in verse with Seth's inimitable charm. The light hearted spirit in which it is written speaks volumes for Seth's state of mind at the time he wrote these tales, a time when he is languishing in the heat of a merciless summer afternoon which it is too hot to concentrate on the more substantial 'A Suitable

Boy'. Being a retelling of fables the themes are essentially social and humanitarian but Seth gives them a subtle twist here and there to make the stories co- temporal in their relevance to the ironies of life.

In *"Beatly tells Here and There"*, there are ten animal fables: two are Seth's original and others are from India, China, Greek and Ukraine. This is written in verbal levity but its themes run deep and serious. Seth evinces his superb art in creating verse from in fables from the tradition of these different countries. These tales are not merely rhymed doggerels, they are structured around the classics tension between good and evil and punctuated by superb illustrations. They appealed as much to children as to adults. This turning of these fables to arts construct as well Seth does without sacrificing the essential vitality of these tales as stories which expressed folk wisdom. The relevance of these folk tales in the context of their primary creations and now all comes to ability to get to certain primal sources of interest in these stories for what they communicate this after being narration or dramatization of human vices, virtues or sentiments together with a keenly amusing perception of animal behavior. In their imaginative freedom these symbols come half way from their sources to meet Seth as he gives them a suitable verse interpretation of beastly behavior is not supplementary to what is human in these poems: it constitutes representations of the complex network of the behavior of man and beast, bird and insect in quasi human terms. The interest which Seth takes to construct upon such behavior accruing from literature and folklore of the past demonstrates his ability to turn to certain sentiments of more than one tradition in this respect. As to milieu of his versification in this respect, it can safely be said that he has moved on to greater artfulness in his use of the sense. Thus in constructing Vishnu Sharma's tale out of the Panchtantra, he does not only create suitable diction for the same, something which brings us to attention with its subtle and direct combination of manners and gestures with available speech as in the cat poems of Eliot or the way Kipling's beats, fowl and reptile use their voices. The tales are evidence of the law of the jingle the good guy does not win, though in *The Monkey and The Crocodile* *"the intended victim outwits"*. They play here to the assembled media and becomes a celebrity despite losing the race, while tortoise fades into obscurity. *"The Elephant and The tragopan"* written by Seth, Features all the animals in a forest bonding together to plead with the local human community not to flood their valley.

Seth has contributed Indian English literature by publishing his another poetic work "Three Chinese poets". It is the final product of Seth's stay in China, In this work Seth offers us his most ambitious and daring translation to date. Though this work is strictly for avid fans of poetry, it is worthwhile to note here how this collection highlights two things namely, Seth's interest in literature and how it takes shape and secondly his conscientiousness as an artist as evinced by the forward to this collection, in which he presents a brief history of T' Ang Dynasty China in order to put the three translated poets into perspective. The three Chinese poets are <u>Wang Wei</u>, <u>Li Bai</u> and <u>Du Fu</u>, who were almost direct contemporaries and lived during the T Ang Dynasty, Translated from the original ideograms (The graphic symbols of Chinese writing system). Seth closely follows the form and subject of the poem in what is a controlled and skillful collection. He writes in the introduction to the volume that his aim as a translator was to be as faithful as possible to the originals, rather than use them as "Trampolines". To bounce his poems off what he has to say about the limitations of translation is interesting given that in *A Suitable Boy,* he represents in English, conversations that have taken place in Hindi, Urdu and Bengali. This work is an evidence not only of his skill as a poet but also his abilities as a linguist and a translator.

Vikram Seth was commissioned by the English National Opera to write a libretto based on the Greek legend of Arion and the Dolphin. The opera was performed for the first time in June 1994. Orion Children's Books subsequently published a picture book based on the opera in which Vikram Seth's words are illustrated by the internationally acclaimed artist Jane Ray. The book has since been made into a twenty-five minute animated special entitled "Arion and the Dolphin" which has shown in Australia, Canada, Iceland, Malta, New Zealand, and throughout the United Kingdom.

The aim of this book is to study "Thematic and Stylistic study of Vikram Seth's Novels". So far he has come out with three novels namely *The Golden Gate (1986),* which is a novel in verse, *A Suitable Boy (1993)* which is a novel of 1349 pages and *An Equal Music* which is his latest novel released in 1999. The book attempts to discuss the gradual Vikram Seth's evolution of themes and techniques of the novels of Vikram Seth.

As I have said earlier that the diversity of themes, the technical innovation and the linguistic virtuosity are the special characteristics of the recent Indian novelists of the writers who show the evidence of a high level of achievement in deploying the language resource. Vikram Seth is undeniably one of the most outstanding writers. Indeed Seth's work shows the marked linguistic consciousness. It is evidenced from the fact that Seth has successfully expressed the typical ethos of America in **The Golden Gate** in perfect American English, that of India in **A Suitable Boy** in Indian English and that of England in **An Equal Music** in flawless British English.

After **The Golden Gate** had been published, Seth decided to write a short piece about India's early years, but labored over *A Suitable Boy* for almost a decade. After writing the first five hundred pages, Seth lost his momentum, feeling that the novel wasn't detailed accurately, and conducted research in India for more than a year while also spending time living in a village and with his family in order to find a way of weaving his intricate story together.

A Suitable Boy is written in a subtle, unobtrusive style which Vikram Seth attributes to his own taste and beliefs. "The kinds of books I like reading are books where the authorial voice doesn't intrude too much — 19th-century novels, and some 20th-century novels as well," Seth said. "They don't try to pull you up with the brilliance of their sentences as much as pull you into a world." Seth further remarked that "with such a large cast of characters, a strong voice would have been too much. Easy writing makes damn hard reading, and I think the opposite is true as well. The book is not more difficult to read than it has to be" (Robinson). True to his word, the novel begins with a statement from Voltaire, "The secret of being a bore is to say everything" (Seth 1).

This novel is set in the political hotbed of India during the post-independence, post-partition decade of the 1950s. This story examines the inner workings and travails of four families, the Kapoors, Mehras, Chatterjis (Hindus) and the Khans (Muslims). Two primary characters in this story are Mrs. Rupa Mehra and Lata, her marriageable but rebellious youngest daughter. Seth is most proud of his vibrant Mrs. Mehra, who is based in part on Seth's grandmother, also named Rupa Mehra, and whom Seth calls "the muse of the project" (Bemrose). Rupa Mehra is a widow whose mission throughout the novel is to take care of her family, and in particular to the search for a husband of suitable, Hindu character for Lata. However, at the same time, Lata is torn by her mother's wishes and her own love for a Muslim boy.

In the background rests the underlying Hindu/Muslim conflict which saturated the period following the independence of both India and Pakistan, and which continues to batter the South Asian subcontinent today. In the novel, conflict occurs between Hindus and Muslims in the fictional city of Brahmpur, where the story is primarily set. Seth sees *A Suitable Boy* as a plea for religious tolerance, among other things. He says, "It is an insult to Hinduism that, these people have hijacked what it means to be Hindu," he said. "It's tolerance, understanding — not just trying to bash your neighbor over the head because he is Muslim. These things need to be said" (Robinson).

Undoubtly, Seth's errorless mastery of the form and verbal art becomes more evident from his expression in several genres like Poetry, Fiction, Travel writing, poetic novel opera and translations. Seth is also very particular about the form of his writing, the use of language of the text and the style of his expression. According to Supriya Karunakaran "stylistically speaking, Vikram Seth is a very conscious craftsman with a purpose, Seth's novel deserves an enquiry from technical point of view".(3) Seth's first novel "The Golden Gate" was published in 1986 when he was 34 years old. It has been composed in verse, having 594 rhyming tetrameter sonnets. In this novel there were 7000 lines that describes the love and life of key characters John, Janet Hawakaya, Phill, Liz and Ed. *Gore Vidal* has called it "The Great California Novel". All the 594 sonnets have been written in Iambic Tetrameter and have followed the fourteen lines stanza pattern of

"Eugene Onegin". <u>The Golden Gate</u> secured Sahitya Akademi Award for Seth in 1988. The theme of the novel is one of the classic materials of all comedy. Man's search for love and the various mishaps that befall him in the course of that search, although the rest of the novel leads less to the traditional comic ending than to surprising sadness. The novel begins from this relatively simple inception and steadily enlarges in scope as it becomes a bitter-sweet love story a wickedly funny novel of manners and a sentiments meditation on morality and nuclear abyss.

John Brown, the hero is a silicon valley computer professional who's highly successful career stands in abysmal contrast to his personal life, which leaves much to be desired when he gets hit hard by a Frisbee while taking a walk he thinks:

"If I died, who'd be sad?

Who'd weep? Who would be glad?

Would anybody?" (4)

This dismal rumination is not in the nature of paranoid self pity. It is a cold blooded evaluation of the state of affairs in John's world. John is an emotional non-entity. Nobody needs him beyond his work and this irks him no end. Beneath all his frivoling capers and his outwards aggressiveness, he has the basic human need to be loved by somebody. He uncomfortably senses that he exists in a vaccum.

The basic theme is thus that of isolation and estrangement. Exploring the alienation in modern American society, Trilling says "The individual is not only isolated from everyone he knows, even his own love partner". (5) Seth unflinchingly presents this melody afflicting modern society. The morbid pre occupation with one's own affairs to the exclusion of everything and everyone else, the selfishness inherent in the non-sharing of thoughts time and needs the stubborn rejection of human bounding in essence, the problem confronting modern urban society is that in it all the things that constitute the very structure of society have been turn down.

"I realized that one could write about one's own times with a modern sensibility and yet use these forms which have existed in the language for hundreds of years, full of the resonance that they had and the clarity that almost forced upon one." (6)

Another theme in the novel is that of nuclear war. Seth expatiates upon the theme unhurriedly, using narration, description, dialogue, sermon demonstrations, and peace marches even diatribe to get the point across. Nuclear insanity is a very contemporary theme and it is very significant in this novel because both the theme and the novel are so quintessentially American. Seth's view point is unequivocal he says in the novel, "nice folks don't use nukes", driving home the fact that such an event spells doom not only for man but also for all of nature's dumb creations who will unwittingly share man's fate.

Another dominant theme in the novel is that of homosexuality, which makes the novel particularly true to the American way of life. Homosexuality is by no means an American Invention but due to its prevalence in American society it has acquired almost a cult state there. Townsend discusses the prevalence of this way of life in America. But the "The Golden Gate" is not an attempt to glorify homosexuality. It is a credit to

Seth's art that he does not the novel glorify homosexuality, nor does he degenerate into a vicious Diatribe against it. Seth's another theme in **The Golden Gate** is that of morality.

He does not subscribe to the concept of conventional Indian morality. As an artist he recognizes the complexities of human nature, unpalatable though they may be. The moral code presented in the novel is the moral code that America lives by: casual sex is a way of life, as are homosexuality relationships, pick up bars and soon social morality, or what one owes to the work at large has been brought to the forefront by the episode of the peaceful demonstration against lung less labs. Seth unambiguously says that "one must look beyond one's personal world to do what one can for society as a whole, emphatically stating "I am my brother's keeper". (7)

The Golden Gate (1986) is the first work that brought Seth's fame and the work was heralded for its European connection and American centred theme. An Indian born poet carries the rich tradition of unmemorable Indian epics, fables and folklores as well as the sonnets in English literature; all seem to unify in the making of this masterpiece. He was noticed not just for the concise and ingenious treatment of the theme i.e. - the existential anguish of the main protagonist but also for the dexterity with which he adhered to the rhyming tetrameter versification.

The Golden Gate thematically depicts romantic passion, materialism, loneliness, alienation, frustration, isolation, disillusionment and discontentment. This novel is a representative and symbolic of modern life in metropolitan cities of the world. It is a tragic love story of modern Americans living in San Francisco, California in 1980s who are called Yuppies. John is the central figure of this novel, a successful young executive of Silicon Valley. Seth portrays that John is an isolated unhappy alienated man in the very opening of the sonnet and novel ends with John's unhappy life. John comes in contact with one of his old friend getting inspiration from whom he places an ad in a local newspaper and after many attempts he succeeds in finding a companion of his choice. His companion Liz Dorati is an intelligent charming lawyer. John's relation with Liz becomes so much deeper. But Liz's brother has a homosexual relationship with John's friend Phill and Liz' priority for her cat who John does not like, becomes the cause of departing this relation and they were separated. This separation becomes the reason of painful environment of loneliness and frustration for John Brown. His mother is no more and his father also doesn't take responsibility of his relation after retirement from government job.

The Golden Gate represents a true Californian character. For the testing when he is invited to become godfather of Liz's child and also he has to face the deaths of so many people with him i.e. the death of his first lover and later friend Janet, Mrs Dorathi and Doctor Hutt Lamont.

The Golden Gate is basically about Californian Diaspora because most of the characters portrayed in the novel by Seth seem to be exploring the vision of reality and illusions already found in the lives of Californians. In this novel, major characters one replaced by minor characters. The reference of Shakespeare's King Lear is seen in sonnet 2.24

through a letter written by Anne T Friese i.e. Janet addressed as 'the king's third daughter'. This is a direct reference of Cordelia, the third and the youngest daughter of King Lear.

Janet is an important character in this novel she is a drummer and chiefly a sceptre by profession. She is in close contact with John. Janet is the only female friend of John is who had steadily devoted to her act during some serious negotiations with him. She always tries to take care of him. So she found a suitable life- companion for John through advertisement. John selects three girls on the advertisement of Janet but finally he selects Elizabeth Dorathi alias Liz with whom he falls in love. Phill is also an important character of this novel. He is John's former roommate and presently his friend. Because of separation from his wife Claire out of misunderstanding, he also lives a lonely life. He attends music concerts organized by Liz and John and Sue is the chief performer. There in the concert he comes in contact with Ed who is Liz's brother. Phill started homosexual relationship but everything has a limit. So that after Liz's separation from John she married Phill.

The other theme of **The Golden Gate** is nuclear warfare. A lengthy segment the novel deals with anti- war demonstration and it deals with the life of America. America is the only country where people are aware enough to protest the acquisition of nuclear weapons the novel shows that Phill who proves as rigid in his sight wing pro-bomb politics as he is in his dislike of Liz's cat, leaves his promising career of nuclear science and joins another job. Liz participates in the anti war demonstration and gives a persuasive speech against the arms race the seventh chapter of the novel is devoted entirely to the protest march against the bomb eighteen sonnets.

Vikram Seth earns a mention as an emigrant Indian, although not strictly one in the limited definition of the term, by various listings of prominent South Asian American amongst whom he is commonly included. Seth's epic fiction *The Golden Gate*, borrows modernism assumptions of ennui and purposelessness into the context of upper middle class. Seth succeeds in showing the gap between romantic, courtly assumptions and culture behind the form against the dull, dry and highly practical life of Yuppies. Seth defends his chosen form as an attempt to raise it the mere 'hudibrastic tricks' to which it has descended but much of Seth's own verse appears to achieve little else.

It is under the structure of Diaspora that we can assemble such different works as **Bye-Bye Blackbird** (Anita Desai, 1971) and **The Golden Gate** and **Wife** (Bharati Mukharji, 1975) Vikram Seth's bridge and his detailed signs of the social and physical landscape constitute structures that simultaneously suggest belonging and distance, continuity and morality of the individual. Seth has tried his utmost to delineate an intimate Californian life style. There are a number of details that range from the seemingly inconsequential to more serious social issues open to debate and contemporary sexual men and nuclear ornaments. Seth enters into the culture of his American world completely and writes about the lives of specific calls of Americans with great cultural aims in teriority making invisible his own Indian self. A borderless and multicultural world is conjured up by the novel by the facts surrounding its inspiration and its author.

In San Francisco, the East and the West do not meet actually they blend. ***The Golden Gate*** shows the relative proximity of the east sharing the same ocean with the west here. Seth paints the city of San Francisco in all its colourful glory, delineating all the minute things that constitute the heart beat of the city and California itself is the place in America for migrant and expatriate multicultural scene. The book is, however, very much a Diaspora narrative seen from the point of view of an Englishman who has gone to Stand ford to get Ph.D and moves in Yuppie circles of second generation Japanese artists. Lastly it can be said that ***The Golden Gate*** is a novel written by an Indian writer Vikram Seth who deals with California, proving it to be a Californian Diaspora as well as American Diaspora

These are various themes that the novel encompasses and they make the novel so much more than a portrayal of contemporary California life. The theme is the outcome of a deep choice. Seth sees the world around him and it pains him. He sees the mindless striving after materialistic goals, the insatiable greed for everything the world has to offer, the ungoverned lust that is more animal like than human the self centeredness, the estrangements from loved ones. But he does not believe in spouting venom against what he perceives as censorious, he is more understanding than being outraged. In a quite manner, he strips the glamour from American Yuppiedom: there is more to this life than sun shine there and California wine- there is loneliness so intense that people build walls around themselves to convince that they are island, there is self-doubt, unrelenting professional pressure, no set of values to live by, confused moral codes and an ever increasing alienation from human touch.

As a novel of plot and character **'The Golden Gate'** is very thin indeed, in essence being little more than a succession of musical beds. To have attempted to render this tale in prose would have produced nothing more than a soap-operatic effect that would hardly have been recognized worthwhile. But the medium of novel is sequential sonnets, by its very nature calls for a certain dignity of approach as well as it demands from Seth an economy of delineation that ruthlessly leaves out the redundant, allows for the witty couplet at the end of each sonnet to break the monotony and most importantly, calls attention away from the plot towards the form. Byron was considered as the pioneer of the novel in verse, his *Don Juan* is a picaresque novel in verse. The style of writing is same as Seth's 'The Golden Gate'. Seth makes this novel interesting by using the tetrameter, "The once noble meter", "capers before the proud pentameter, tyrant of English". However though the pentameter is no doubt stately and grand, the tetrameter has a lilting cadence that must have appealed to Seth's musical ear. Like Seth's style of writing consists of about four hundred sonnets, written in Iambic Tetrameter, the rhyming pattern being: Ababa cdcd efef gg. The octave and sestet are usually well defined, although Pushkin leaps across to the next sonnet occasionally to complete a sentence or a thought. Seth has also written in this form that even the acknowledgement, the dedication and the table of contents have been versified. The opening line is arresting for its humorous dig at the lengthy epic style of Yore: which

Seth knows the average modern reader is not likely to read.

The sonnet form is harnessed by Seth in a manner that oscillates from being merely functional in taking the story forward to being rich in poetic eloquence. In the present novel Seth uses the broader base of fiction to unite the two genres of fiction and poetry. By using the stanziac form innovatively, he "attempts an imaginative and creative union of two genres so crudely pulled asunder by earlier and writers". This blending is conscious and careful. Realizing the advantages verse wields over prose, Seth uses it to communicate his experiences effectively. This has the added advantage of enabling Seth to use a medium in the nature of a vital artistic evolution leading to a more heightened expression of experience than prose. Seth has chosen the Title of special import, because the name 'The Golden Gate' captures the quit siring of modern California. It stands as defining features of America's west coast, just as the statue of liberty is the defining feature of the eastern one. In the novel, Seth uses the bridge to indicate the identifying landmark of San Francisco. It becomes the novel's raison d'etre as well, becoming the majestic backdrop of the human drama that unfolds. The bridge which is used by Seth in this novel becomes a symbol of love, representative of the soul test of worthiness, which all the characters must travel before being late into the sanctum sanctorum of the kind of love they have only ever dreamed about, never known.

After completion of '*The Golden Gate*' Seth published his novel 'A Suitable Boy' in 1993. Seth got Commonwealth Writer's Prize in 1994 for this work. Through this work, Seth created literary history with the books mammoth size and the million copies' sales. 'A Suitable Boy' is a carefully researched account of political and social life in India after independence: its action climaxes in 1952 a year the book terms "auspicious". In this novel Seth combines satire and romances to even greater effect that it becomes one of the most popular narratives of the late twentieth century. Amazon.Com review says, "The book is a delight, at once touching, humorous and widely panoramic. It is really several novels in one. The novel is full of rich and detailed accounts of

India and everything Indian". The classic realism of 'A Suitable Boy' was for many readers of Indian fiction in English, a welcome break from the musical realism of the other heavy weight author from the subcontinent, Salman Rushdie.

'A Suitable Boy' 'centers on the motif of a young woman's quest for love which in these disillusioned times has become s lost thread. The young heroine of the novel, Lata, faces a dilemma over which suitor she should select. Three suitors represent three paths in human life. The novel is endowed with human appeal. The novelist goes back to the early fifties for artistic effect. It is the undeniably threaded with a love and marriage plot, but is almost as concerned, intricately so, with the economics of village life, the impact of land reform legislation on cities and villages and effect of local currency based on chits. It also discusses movingly and persuasively, on the after- shocks of the 1947 India Pakistan partition and the day to frictions of religious conflict same as Salman Rushdie's 'Midnight Children', The event happens to the Seth family too who being Hindus, left Pakistan just

before partition. Seth's plot resolutions in 'A Suitable Boy' as in his other books do not always follows conventional expectations. "True Love often doesn't win", Seth says: "there are other things, and they do impinge on people, I can't take the view that you can live on love and fresh air". (8)

Seth's technique of writing in this novel 'A Suitable Boy' has been compared with the Nobel laurate, Nagnib Mahfouz's 'The Cairo Trilogy, or *Leo Tolstoy's war and peace* or Marcel Proust's 'Remembrance of Things Past'. Seth's technique also brings to one's mind the technique employed by Jane Austen and George Eliot. Seth's narrative technique is never heavy or dull even when he is describing the drudgeries of Indian politics. It is written large with imaginative sympathy and organic sensibility. Pico Iyer wrote in 'The Times Literary Supplement' that every page of the novel is readable and true and believes that Seth has reinvented English literature. Trevol Fishlock who reviewed the book for 'Sunday Telegraph' is of the view that it is invested with truly Gangetic quality, it is a fiction on a grand scale. Seth's handling of the institution of marriage is generous and untypical, and there are little of the darker aspects of Indian marriage life.

The literary tradition Seth has inherited is essentially western and so the Russian literary model adds **War and Peace** to *Eugene Onegin* and blends it with the Victorian model named in the novel itself **Middle March** Literary allusions are employed from Austen, Flaubert, E.M Forster and Eliot, Seth's use of pastiche enables him to intensify the character delineation. Jane Austen's style and Seth's style have been compared. Seth shares Austen's level headed approach towards marriage, reiterating that plain common sense should govern one's actions rather than Romantic visions although a fusion of the two would be tolerant and too fond of his character to want to transform them.

Seth's technique in this novel involves conjuring up a brilliant sense of the comic, evident especially when he writes about the Chatterjees and their circle. The overwhelming atmosphere of the novel is one of tongue-in-cheek humor, despite the occasional dark storm clouds that gather. It is as if Seth is exhorting the reader to dwell on the tragic ones, aware that reducing one's problem to the playful silliness of kakoli-couplets will rob them of some of their gravity. Seth also seeks to divest the Indian holy men and gurus of their mystic spirituality as the majority of them really are opportunists. The Swamis and the gullibility of their devotees provide some highly comic scenes in the novel. Seth's use of language in the novel is also unique, because **A Suitable Boy** is the only work in Seth's canon that occasions an examination of language, flawless English but with such an Indian subject, a tale written in unadulterated English would perhaps not have been so convincing, apart from being less opposite as well. The Indianism in **A Suitable Boy** is confined to middle class society.

An Equal Music (1999) is Seth's third novel set in London with classical western music in its background. Seth combines the story of love with music, passion and the culture of musicians. The musician Michael Holden, is the protagonist of the novel and this novel centres on his life. The socio-cultural concept combines two main fields: society and culture. Community involves a group of people who are the members of various societies, and culture is the conduct of the community as a whole. European performers, musicians, singers all move very swiftly from one location to another. Vikram Seth depicts his characters along with their culture, tradition and celebration.

Seth explains Michael's and Julia's miserable and lonely lives while Michael wanted to live with Julia. She did not like Nora in A Doll's House and wants to severe the familiar connection. Julia still keeps up with her culture and adheres to limitations, though she is a modern woman. The lovers did not cross the limitation of culture. Julia's married life awakes her to behave in a proper manner. The life of Michael was very disturbed because of the separation. However Michael and Julia are usually bound in this situation, their culture would not allow them to behave like lovers

In *An Equal Music* Seth depicts British culture by setting London and Vienna. Seth does not try to criticize the country which had once colonized his motherland. In this novel Michael is the second violinist with muggier quartet. The novel deals with how Michael reacts when he finds his lost love and becomes a lonely person. Michael and Julia firstly meet in Vienna where both were studying music. Seth draws a picture here of two lovers from different places as student and return after a long period of ten years. They became significant musicians in Vienna and London. Seth also shows their vicissitudes as classical musicians where in English schools classical music is taught and chamber music is losing its appeal and string quartets finds it difficult to survive. This novel is written after much research by Seth and this is evident in the minute's details about turnings of structuring a performance of violin maker, of the heated arguments amongst the characters regarding nuances of their performance. Seth's novels are written in Diasporic elements.

The migration can be seen in *An Equal Music* where Michael moves away from his hometown into the countryside to Vienna and then to the city of London to pursue a musical career. The character takes up a cosmopolitical identity rather than a pan-national identity. This is one of the traits of Diaspora. Seth also moves from one country to another country. He grew up in India and he had travelled as he was a student at Oxford in Britain, Stand Ford in America and Nanjing University in China. His works reflects his in- depth knowledge of these different countries.

An Equal Music reveals Vikram Seth's fondness for irony That Michael happens to be Batcher's son is itself ironic. Seth approaches to social reality helps the novel to set its foot in the real world of man. When Michael describes the changes in Rochdale, he serves his creator's role of a social critic. In this novel Seth has created a living, breathing world that enchants and grips the readers and a love- epic of Michael and Julia. Seth has presented discontinuous lovers meeting after a long period and they established physical relationship despite Julia's being married to James. But sexuality is acceptable neither to Seth nor to society. Vikram Seth portrays the lifestyle of the young people with responsibility dream, passion, love, pain and sacrifice. Seth is also interested in exploring western culture and classical music which evokes the nation's cultural prosperity and he successfully depicts the diasporic elements in his novels like *An Equal Music* and *The Golden Gate*

Vikram Seth is one of those human beings privileged and fortunate enough to be able to travel and make the world their own; a peripatetic lifestyle has moulded the themes and shapes of most of his work. As Seth says "I have been quartered between California, China, India and England." But Seth interested in these four cultures in not that of a detached observer context merely to portray the exotic, It rather that of audios, interested learner trying to arrest the essence of them all. C.Vijayshree points out:

> "Seth's work reveals the response of an expansive Indian sensibility to the richness of varied cultures outside: alternate points of view, or disapprove divergences."(9)

Seth takes time out to absorb a foreign culture before venturing to write about it and consequently, his works always bear the stamp of authenticity, no matter how alien is the locale. Even in the case of the novel **A Suitable Boy** which is purely Indian in theme. Seth did not treat the subcontinent as his favourite. The fact that he was an Indian did not make him intrinsically qualified to write about India. In an interview with Nona Walia, Seth said:

> "There's challenge to the way you tell a story every time. I am obsessive about the process of writing, it has to be perfect. The challenge is emotional and structural. It's about how you tell story, exploring the various possibilities of that book, the order and path it takes and how you allow the book to take its natural course........ I go where my stories take me. I try to tell things as they are."

Thus Seth manages to write his brilliant books that seen to come from address different locations. If *The Golden Gate* is 'pure' California, *A Suitable Boy* is north India and *An Equal Music* is from Europe.

Seth's **An Equal Music,** is an extraordinary novel about music and love, culled from his experience of chamber music in England. The book in 400 pages captures life in musical London just as saw the earlier novels illumined India and California. **An Equal Music** is another romantic novel by Seth, but this time without the satire of '**A Suitable Boy'.** Seth presents an emotionally rich and brilliantly penned novel set in the world of European classical music circuit. It is a sensitive story about unrequited love and struggle between desire and duty, between sound and silence. The story centers to the reignited love affair of a violinist with a gifted young pianist who is going deaf. As in **The Golden Gate** there is still consolation to be found outside oneself: in friendship and natural world. In this novel, there is in addition music, which transfigures those who play it and which 'is a sufficient'. Seth describes the claustrophobic social world of a string quartet, their rehearsals, performances and psychology of their relationships with each other.

By turn elegiac and witty, '**An Equal**

Music' introduces the readers to another facet of Vikram Seth's unique talent. It marks a breaking away from Seth's earlier self controlled and distanced style of writing. The reason for this becomes clear when Seth reveals that for him music acts as a refuse from the tensions of work and he found it difficult to reconcile himself to the thought of writing about it. Music amounts to a passion, almost an obsession with Seth. And this is evident from the style in which **'An Equal Music'** has been written so different from Seth's previous work, as he strives to capture the essence of music in words. Seth says:

> "I am very close
> to music in some ways, closer
> then to words. If I had to
> choose whether to have
> music on a desert isle or
> words no question I would
> choose music." (10)

In **'An Equal Music'** Seth similarly endeavors to make comprehensible and accessible to the reader a world in which music is the theme that unites lives. There is some kind of music in every page: it even insinuates itself into the love story, providing the ethereal framework over which the fragile gossamer threads of love story are woven. Every musician will gasp at what Seth has been about to discern and express, for his ability to translate the sounds of music into the written words is astounding. Seth had great knowledge about the chamber music classics of the Viennese school; In this respect '**An Equal Music**' has an almost canonical approach to the classical music repertoire.

In antipodal contrast to Salman Rushdie who tackles the same theme of music and love in **The Ground beneath Her Feet**, Seth does not depict the life of musicians in a fog of bombastic glee and music realism. His writing is close to the bones, the private and public life of musician in quarter, Seth's own empathy for classical music given an irresistible depth of tone to the narrative. "I am the trout the angler, the brook, the observer", (11) he tells us as he plays Schubert: as the muggier rehearse, vacillating from impatience with each other to musical perfection, Seth deftly narrates the joys of collabiration, trust and creation. Even the technical difficulties encountered by a string quarter in playing certain pieces are explored in depth as for instance the needs to tone down a viola in order to play Bach's **The Art of the Fugue.**

It is true that **'An Equal Music'** is substantially technical and can therefore be potentially distracting for every non- musically aware reader. However Seth categorically states that he writes primarily for the reader who knows what he is talking about. It is the situation where he gains some readers and loses some with each work. But the wide acclaim both **'A Suitable Boy'** and **'An Equal Music'** have received is testimony to their excellence as art form.

In **'An Equal Music'**, alienation has been delineated as natural part of life With the passage of time; it naturally develops and makes its presence more conspicuous, thereby manifesting its pervasiveness. Loneliness is omnipresent in Seth's novels. It can be also seen in **'An Equal Music'** The character Michael can be seen as a lonely person in the very first paragraph:

"The   branches
are bare, the sky tonight a
milky violet. It is not quiet
here, but it is peaceful. The
wind ruffles the black water
towards me. There is no one
about. The birds are still. The
traffic slashes through Hyde
Park. It comes to my ears as
white noise. I test the bench
but do not sit down. As
yesterday, as the day before, I
stand until I have lost my
thoughts." (12)

*(Vikram Seth, An Equal Music, New Delhi
Penguin 1999 P-3)*

We distinguish the familiar sadness of the
lonely man who has been trapped in empty situation.
Micheal after the separation with Julia starts playing
Violin in the quartet where through sheer lust and
loneliness he maintains unsatisfying love affair with
his music student Virginie. Michael says: "She wants
it to, and I go along with it, through lust and

loneliness". (13) Love affair does not change the things for Michael. However, he meets Julia after ten years and both feel overjoyed to see each other nevertheless; the feeling of alienation becomes the part of their life. They are chased and haunted continuously by alienation. Alienation persists even in the company of Julia. However, Michael suffers more from it when Julia leaves him for good.

Vikram Seth wants to cast the fact of contemporary life that whether one is surrounded by chatterer or smiler, whether one reads books in the crowded bus; one is in the lonely majority. Almost all the characters are lonely and for most part of their lives. The feeling of loneliness is omnipresent in Seth's fiction. Alienation is there the lives of John, Michael. Sheeda bai is symbolic of man's existential loneliness in the universe, Seth's marvelous sense of place, which entails in this instance the ability to conjure up visual spaces through aural cues. Seth has the knack for bringing a place to life by homing in on its uniqueness and in what the place sounds like: the rising song of a lark evokes the moors of Rochdale; London is represented by the songs of robins in winter and blackbirds in summer and by pigeons, Vienna is conjured up by the sound of nightingales, and Venice by the music of Vivaldi. . Seth thus authenticates the novel by linking the profession of the characters with their ironic perception of world.

In '**An Equal Music**', music is not only instrumental music but also music in life, hence harmonious relationships. Just as music is created out of fusion of euphonic sounds, so is the case of authentic life that can come into existence only with fusion of two perspectives, aims and perceptions. Hence, disharmonious music results in meaningless life. Seth's first person narrator and the quartet's second violinist, Michael is to some extend an outsider. He does not belong to London by birth, nor is he of a musical background. He grew up in Rochdale, the son of a small businessman and had to work against his parent's prejudice as well as that of the more privileged people he encounters in musical circles. Rochdale His confidence in himself and his abilities are always governed by his sense that he does quite belong as well as his knowledge that nor does his fit in back in Rochdale either. This sense of displacement echoes back to the themes Seth explores in **A Suitable Boy.**

At the concluding point of view Seth's fictional world is a human comedy of love sought and lost and beloved found and lost. And so Seth's novels always end in disappointment. Seth's men and women are victims of controlled desire. Being highly emotional and sensitive, they pursue passionate relationship in which they fail. Seth seems to convey through these passionate characters the fact that passion transforms the individual into suffering, despair and destruction. Those who are smeared in outrageous and passionate actions are sure to be met with displeasure. The youthful love and mutual attraction are generally not the basis of enduring relationship which is the realization of the characters of Seth. These passionate characters find it very difficult to conform to the norms of the society but after their failure they are obliged in the end to conform to the patterns of the middle class rules.

'**An Equal Music**' is thus a departure from Seth's earlier work. It represents a sort of coming of age as Seth replaces the partly ironic and humors treatment he usually accords to love with intensity, almost a compulsion to explore its more serious side. It can be undoubted said that Seth is quite practical when it comes to treat love as is evident from his earlier works where he always seems to tell the reader to take love at its face value and not to give it more importance than it actually deserves aside as he discovers and articulates what it means to be so passionately in love, whether with a person or with an art form. Daniel Johnson has praised **An Equal Music** as "The finest novel ever written about music in English" and Maggie Gee wrote "Seth gives the fullest portrait I have ever read in fiction of a musician's relationship to his music". (14)

The novel thus reiterates Seth's earlier philosophy of the value of such mundane institutions as home and family. It is a story about the ultimate triumph of sanity over human irrationality, and seeking to create a balance between personal and artistic worlds. It explores loneliness especially the loneliness of an artist and seeks to portray the interface of creativity with the unavoidable tensions of daily life. It is also about the joy of having regained what was thought to be lost forever, coupled with the anguish of realization and denial. It is impassioned and poetic, elegiac and witty by turns and set against the Augustan backdrop of Venice and Vienna, obvious passion for his subject and his subsequent empathy with it lend this novel an extra dimension. Lastly, we can say that, this together with his talent for words and imagery and an excellent literary ending makes this novel an exceptional read.

Vikram Seth published his another book **Two Lives** (2005); whose he turned his obsessional eye on his uncle and aunt. It is the first very personal non fictional work he has even written. Twentieth century saw one of the most vicious genocides in human history, the terrifying scenes of man persecuting fellow human beings, for having been born in a star crossed religion. What happened to the luck less creators aimed in this massive manhunt and who escaped the gas chamber has been occasionally recorded but rarely with the tone of self lost wonderment that pervades **Two Lives.** Seth chronicles a couple who married rather late in life but made their marriage endure in spite of all the complexity that surrounded their union. This work belonged to Seth's great uncle, Shanty Behari Seth (1908-1994) and his great aunt Henny Gorda (1908-1989). Seth went to live with them in London, when he was in bording school at Tombridge., They announce themselves with urgency to him that he cannot resist. Before his aunt and uncle died he knew he would have to write about them. "He says that there was something in the freedom to examine a life in full that attracted him, as well as the intrinsic power of their story." (15)

Seth's uncle was a Hindu from India who went Berlin to study medicine and settled down in London as a dentist. He had to go through the agony of losing his right arm while fighting the German troops at Monte Casino, but continued to practice until his retirement. Seth's aunt was a Jew from Germany who escaped in 1939, hounded out by Hitler's genocide to seek safety in England. She had the psychological pressure of leaving behind her mother and sister in hostile Germany. Seth has spent much of the past six years trying to reconstruct their remarkable marriage from letters and memories and interviews he conducted with his uncle before his death.

Seth's work is characterized by the innovative recuperation of "unfashionable" and "traditional" forms such as the realist roman- fleauve and a novel in verse. Such recuperation goes against the current of cross pollination between genres and stylistic and technically experimentation which characterizes other writers like Salman Rushdie or Amitabh Ghosh, to whom he is always compared. Seth experiences the sense of an old fashioned conception of the relationship between reader and writer. Engaging the attention and interest of the "common reader" becomes a programmatic element of the both his poetry and his prose, and his books reveal a sophisticated yet oneself conscious return to realist narrative and formal poetic structures. A presentation of Seth's work does not easily yield an organic picture, since he has radically changed not only genre but also setting nearly every book he was written. Such diversity makes tracing the evolution (thematic) of Seth's output difficult and less relevant than it would be to a more homogeneous oeuvre. Nevertheless there are curtain threads which run through his work, starting from his collection of poetry.

Seth is indisputably one of the most important of Indian writers. His fiction has achieved a remarkable place in the fictional world. He is an interesting member of the parliament of Indian poets in English, where traditional Indian poets in English have proffered verses of sorrow and tones unremitting gloom although Dom Moraes, K.N. Daruwala, Shankar Mokashi Punekar, M.K Naik and Nissim Ezekiel, have occasionally tried their hand at witty light verse. Seth has managed to strike a whole new tone. Seth combines the irony of Ezekiel the acerbity of Daruwalaand the attention to form of Mokashi Punekar and produces what is surely some of the best humorous and casual verse in contemporary Indian poetry. Seth is an effusive, versatile writer; in whose mind many novel ideas must be germinating and many more writings will emerge, in future days to come. Seth truly infringes the geographical, historical and poetical divisions through his yearning to reach out to several cultures so as to create a harmonious zone. His writings have undoubtly helped him create a place for himself; it has yielded him a comfortable place to discover and explore many more horizons. Seth shows the foresightedness by combining tradition with modernity in all his novels. The underlying theme of all his novels becomes negation of passion in all forms with emphasis on tolerance and simple and chaste life. Seth as a humorist and a realist manages to bring in light descriptions to subdue the seriousness prevailing. A novel gets the status of a literary classic if the novelist gives appropriate expression through a language suited to it. Seth has done admirable work in presenting authentic characters convincing situations permeating the rich network of the novel through suitable language suiting different mind sets and conditions. Moreover, Seth is conscious of giving suitable sensibility to the particular novel. Seth apart from giving authenticity to the appropriate dialect of different regions through linguistic differences gives a picture of stagnation in the academic field too where a scholar's zeal to show creativity gets fast extinguished. Seth negates the state of passion in all forms that destroys and cripples one's sanity. All of Seth's novel reveal the underlying theme i.e. rejection of passion. Clearly, the answer to Seth's remarkable diversity of both apprehending and expressing lies in this attitude he holds towards the creative process. This tendency to be receptive to different experiences and suggestions would appear to serve the artist quite well. But the imagination heads something concrete to work upon, and in this respect Seth willingly obliges, leaving no stone unturned for his research on any aspect of his choice of theme. For **A Suitable Boy**, he devoted a year exclusively to research, and for '**An Equal Music**' he attended classes for the deaf, attended their music rehearsals, even lived with musicians, in order to apprehend every aspect of his subject to the utmost.

Seth is highly knowledgeable about the greater chamber- music classics of the Viennese school, which is revealed in '**An Equal Music**'. His awe and passion for this classics is evident and firmly precludes music that is post classical in this respect, '**An Equal Music**' has an almost canonical approach to the classical music repertoire. Seth's novel is faithful to all pleasing things in the original: his rhymes stun, expressing within them the entire gamut of human emotions love, hate ambition, agreed, lust sympathy, dejection and novel grows deeper in meaning with every reading previously veiled nuances of its technical virtuosity coming to light. Even in the case of novel as Indian in theme as **A Suitable Boy,** Seth did not take on the subcontinent before he was aware that just the fact that he was an Indian did not make him intrinsically qualified to write about India. He does not try to constantly force the reader to appreciate his command over language and his approach to fiction is unselfconsciously anti modernist. **A Suitable Boy** is accessible to the general reader even at 1300+ pages that even when it ends, the reader has not had enough and wants to know what happens next.

Seth's eclectic reading has made tremendous impact on his own literary tastes and beliefs, and consequently on his art. His style is highly allusive and behind this is the wealth of earlier literature, Chaucer, The Elizabethans, The Romantics, The Poetry of Hardy, T' ang dynasty Chinese poets and so on. Seth says about his literary preferences:

"The kind of books I like reading are books where the authorial voice doesn't intrude too much like the nineteenth century novels, and some twentieth century novels, as well. They don't try to pull you up with the brilliance of their sentences as much as pull you into a world." (16)

These would be the novelists like Jane Austen, George Eliot and R.K. Narayan whom Seth by self –confession cannot resist reading. He is an open admirer of R.K. Narayan and describes him as "a wonderful writer, the greatest of us all." (17)

Seth's recreation of the world which always appears true, whether he is writing a story about west coast America, post independence India, or the world of European classical music circuit. However Seth believes like Goethe that the artist works in real in so far as it is always true: ideal in that it is never actual. Seth is an accomplished artist and treads with considerable poise this fine line rendering the near and the familiar with artistic verisimilitude. Pico Iyer groups narayan, Seth and Rohinton Mistry togetherin one strand of Indian English fiction which he terms "compassionate realism". He opposes to this the stand of "pin wheeling invention" to which he claims Rushdie, Shashi Tharoor, and I. Seth's place in Indian English fiction, it seems, is constantly defined by the contrast he provides to Rushdie. Whereas **Rushdie's Midnight Children** uses the fantastic in the tradition of magic realism, Seth is realistic while Rushdie draws attention to his language; Seth's prose is clear and easy and as Pico Iyer words:

"Seth is a pacemaker where Rushdie is a belligrem." (18) Seth's attempt has been to free the contemporary novel of its seriousness, its contempt for the simple passion, its increasingly academic concerns with critics and deconstructionists. He wants to make literature undoubting and accessible for the general reader. He believes that an over emphasis on style and modernist techniques has diverted writing from its original course. Seth says:

"I don't read a lot of modern fiction but it seems to me that too much of it is their fodder. Since the rise of the academic critic, writing has had to have an increased sophistication, as if subjects such as the airport novel, writers come out of university courses and carry into their writing academic concerns rather than the concerns of the general reader." (19)

This concern for the general reader makes his work so approachable. Seth's approach to fiction is unselfconsciously anti modernist and he does not force upon the reader to appreciate his command over language. Seth is one of those human beings privileged and fortunate enough to be able to travel and make the world their own. A peripatetic life style has moulded the themes and shapes of most of his work.

Vikram Seth is among the crop of bold new writers. His impingement on the condition of Indian English literature in the eighties was in consonance with the larger development of Indian literature at that time. First of all Indian English literature acquired much greater credibility in the one hand and much larger public reception. Secondly it came to be reckoned as an important part of Indian Literature as a whole which was not the case before when Indian English literature was largely viewed as somehow away from the mainstream of Indian literature. Seth benefited from this change in perspective. His novels and poetry grew from a mind integral with Indian conditions of living. And yet it felt equally comfortable with conditions abroad. One remembers his admission that whenever he writes on anything at whatever the place may be, he gets immersed in the place and natural available there. This is particularly true to his novels.

Seth's credits lie in integrating in complementary relevance and signification. In this Seth's creative achievement is almost unique not only in Indian English literature, but also in Indian literature as a whole. An outward movement where a new gets naturalized wherever one goes that is Seth's special achievement an intellectual brilliance as well as perspective that are rare in Indian writing in English. Seth's writing have two directions, one towards India and related to India, where he got national recognition from Sahitya Academy, India's national Academy of letters, along with such other distinguished writers as Amitabh ghosh, Shashi Deshpande and Upamanyu Chatterjee. Seth was first person of his generation to receive such an honor. The other direction is towards the Indian Diaspora where he merits comparison with such writers as Salman Rushdie, Amit chaudhary and Jhumpa Lahiri. Seth's writing, shows a remarkable inwardness, and in both his achievement is extremely worthwhile.

Seth has himself offered explanations of how and why he writes what he does, in a number of interviews which fore grounded personal and familiar identities, socio-political contexts, as also processes of border crossing. Seth has repeatedly disputed demands made of a writer to inject the right amount of 'Indianess' into his work. Seth is aware that he belongs to a particular class of economically privileged Indians who are already alienated to some degree even prior to migration outside the Indian subcontinent, and he succinctly captures the' nowhereness' of this class of Indians who will suffer to some extent of deracination where ever they are. A close thematic analysis of the novel however makes it clear that although Seth adopts a humanist middle ground, he is also well aware of disparate elements that have begun to challenge the centralizing authority of Nehru's ideal of a socialist and secular nation state. Seth's thesis is that 'The future of the secular and socialist ideals of the Indian nation- states lies in the hands of few good men who recognize their duty towards the larger society.' And make a conscious choice to act ethically.

Vikram Seth is an extremely versatile writer, Novelist, poet and translator he has had a worldwide reputation. Seth is an Indian by birth but lived and educated in different countries where he spent his progressive period of time. Seth adds multicultural milieu to his artistic skills which has helped him to bring his English writing to the stage of world literature. Seth has experienced a significant amount of intercultural mobility. Seth has lived in three countries and has written a variety of literary works. As a true classical realist Seth relies on middle class characters and their sensibilities and due importance is given in lower strata and working – class sections of the people at appropriate positions in the novel. Seth adopts his own version of realism to represent the politically servile, economically deprived and socially circumscribed post independent Indian society. His first novel, *The Golden Gate* emerged as a new comer in the stream of Indo English literature. In *The Golden Gate* Seth depicts American culture, living style of people, customs and their mentality. His fictional world is multi dimensional and multi-layered. For Vikram Seth the world is like a stage and its people his characters no matter to which nation and background they belong Seth has never restricted to themes of cultural displacement, search for roots or diasporas dislocations but is a universal writer and writes as the muse takes him Seth's works reach an audience beyond geographical and ideological boundaries.

Seth's *An Equal Music* (1999) comes under the category of international literature. It is a realistic fictional adventure in verse medium and adheres to all the features of social realism. Through this novel Seth eschews his localized status and Seth himself as a writer of translational identity. The story runs through London, Vienna and Venice but the essence of the novel is music. It is story of musician Michael Holme and his recovery of the self. This novel is the depiction of the philosophy of universal humanism. The novel does not talk about the cultural gaps or explore the issue of ambivalence. Rather *An Equal Music* could be read as an attempt to interconnect different boundaries of nationalism. Vikram Seth is a cultural traveller who enjoys his experience of having multiple homes. He is a universal writer and is honest enough to follow his inspiration.

1. (C) Seth's Technique of Writing

Seth's technique of prose writing never loses its charm and poise: nor does he lose his sense of humor and wit and where there is pathos, Seth is supreme. However, despite the pervading gloom and grim picture of mankind his tolerant outlook and appeal for human logic balances it. Undoubtedly, the easy wit and subtle irony mingled with humor in his works well explains the innate goodness and the magnanimity of the author, who by and large reveals an extremely patient and tolerant outlook in all his works. Seth is a writer of the world who is essentially a creative artist of the global world, a craftsman to reckon with popular writer with perhaps the greater readership among the second generation Indo-Anglican writers. Seth with an opportunity to display his wit makes the novels irresistibly funny. The paradox is that the story is not light- toned- only its treatment such but it is not in Seth's repertoire to churn out page after page of unyielding gravity. Seth's style cannot be detached from his humor. It becomes clear that the froufrou atmosphere that Seth conjures up is an effective medium, especially in a novel in which a severe treatment of the course of events could only have resulted in an unbearably heavy tale. By being comic Seth alleviates the gloom of the dire sequence of events, simultaneously paving the way for his exposition on nuclear issu1es and the value of friendship and family.

Vikeam Seth's exclusiveness is largely due to his traditional outlook that has made many critics compare him with reputed writers like Jane Austen and Leo Tolstoy. An in-depth analysis of Seth's art contrives to show his art bearing resemblance to those of the literary giants like Chaucer and Shakespeare. Above all he is an Indian who must have drawn substantially on the influences of Indian classical poets whose epics <u>Ramayana</u> and <u>Mahabharata</u> are all time favorites. Thus the entire gamut of his work in the Indo- European tradition makes him unparallel English authors for years to come.

In **A Suitable Boy**, Seth sketches the post colonial India in 1950's. This comprises the feudal lords, the urban, the rural middle and lower class, as well as the elite, ultra- modern hypocritical Indians who have proudly imbibed the English life. Post colonial writers have always targeted Anglicize characters for their attack and Seth, being no exception, does it with great adroitness, candor in his representative cheek in tongue humorous style, in presenting Chatterjee family who are on eot the most brilliant caricatures ever created by a novelist. Seth not only chooses the Indian lexicons and characters for his Indian tales but for the America and European backdrop too, he succeeds in creating appropriate sensibilities. The central character in California society in *The Golden Gate* is a solitary melancholic character, much unlike the Indian protagonist in *A Suitable Boy* inextricably linked to the large community, the clan and the family tree they belong to Seth quite successfully appears to combine Chaucer's skill at depicting the variety of human nature along with his understanding of men of all ranks. In addition, he also seems to have inherited Chaucer's technical brilliance in the metrical handling of language Chaucer had an unfinished opus *The* **Canterbury** *Tale* that for all times remain a classic example of brilliant tales depicting contemporary social events and atmosphere. Seth accomplished it more extensively in *A Suitable Boy* and to some extent in *The Golden Gate.* Chaucer's characters meet at a pilgrimage while Seth's modern characters of different families and segments of society meet in a marriage party in *A Suitable Boy.* Seth becomes a unique artist in the modern time whose versatility takes us back to the rich treasure of literature. Being an avid reader and scholar, he seems to be aware of different trends in writing viz, fables, and ballad translations etc. like literary giants Chaucer, Shakespeare and T.S.Eliot, Seth too has attempted translations of fables and also of some Chinese poetry without losing the regional lexicon and flavor of the original poetry. He tried other neglected genre, a libretto. In 1994, he was commissioned by the English national opera to write a libretto based on Greek legend of 'Arion and the Dolphin'. The opera was shown in Australia, Canada, Iceland, Malta and Newzealand and throughout the U.K. Thus in Vikram Seth one finds a multi- faceted personality. Indo-Anglican writing got a new lease of life at the hands of promising second generation writers in 1980's such as Salman Rushdie, Vikram Seth and Arundhati Roy They created a furor by hitting the international market by claiming a whooping 26 million to 50 million dollar for their books. Both were nominated for the prestigious Booker Prize for *A Suitable* Boy and *The* God *of* **Small** *Things* respectively. Today they are not only rich; they are the cynosure of critics as well as readers. They have succeeded in performing transnational and cross- cultural communication which have given recognition to a new Indian sensibility and confidence.

Seth excels as a wonderful satirist and his art will be seen combining the wit, depth, tongue in cheek humor of Dryden and Pope of the seventeenth century and also of Jonathan Swift. Seth also appears to be influenced by Jane Austen and George Eliot in projection of moral vision, which Austen depicted through her "two inches of Ivory" small world and what George Eliot revealed through the characters of different professions, forming a microcosm of man in the world. Seth uses Jane Austen's small compact world for ***The Golden Gate*** and later in ***An Equal Music*** and bigger Canvas of **A Suitable Boy.** Perhaps, very few authors would be so versatile to combine the style of Victorian novelists and that too with such flexibility in all three novels. The association with simplicity, constancy and fidelity: inter-relationships emanating from the moral and spiritual presence of nature too will be observed. Seth can be compared to Lawrence for the fact that like Lawrence his belief in instinctive reactions appears to be motivated by morality and spirituality. Lawrence too takes refuge in passion, while Seth upholds it, but the guiding force is the same for both; both intend to show disregard for a mechanized life.

Seth's views are by and large inspired by those of Victorian writers who saw greater good in a patient, poised approach towards stability in society which has already known, emanate a from healthy inter- personal relationships. The emphasis of George Eliot or Jane Austen on fidelity and chastity in love and marriage was but an implication of a larger vision, the betterment of society which in turn would lead to a healthier nation. Seth's turning back to older writers for his story line as well as style proves how much he agrees to their approach which though looks simple and unambitions, the response on the other hand is more unanimously agreeable.

Seth's writing has scholarly knowledge and intuitivism which go in hand into reveal his inner thoughts, his tolerant, calm and poised approach revealed through his traditional approach made him a preferred writer among those making experiments with language and style. Seth has great political awareness, which is one of the lesser prominent aspects of his writing and yet, his respects for his and yet, his response to the prevalent politics of the nation is inevitable. Seth uses this in clauses of politics, in his novels, that needs highlighting for thematic purpose, it also becomes a symbolic and metaphorical allusion. Like Austen, Seth intends to uphold the restrictions imposed on woman in the patriarchal society regarding stereotypical notions of the masculine and feminine. Just as Austen, the social novelist focused on the interaction of individuals and groups within clearly defined community and hoping to reconcile the demands of self and society. Seth's **A Suitable Boy** too contrives to establish a social and moral order where the interests of all are contemplated, irrespective of gender, caste, religion and social divide. The consolidation of such diverse issues is again through Austen's central subject such as marriage, the most important institution that determines the development or deterioration of society and in turn the nation.

Seth preferred the verse form when he found the subject burdensome. It undoubtedly establishes his unique flair for spontaneous poetry that only a few gifted can boast of possessing. And this fact is proved again and again as one goes through the couplets he has written in the beginning of all his novels, including the Two Lives. Seth has also presented the animal theme as a symbol consisting part of an intricate pattern In The Golden Gate as he uses a cat, Ignanaand Schwarzenegger in comic form, through larger than life implication where a kinship between man and animal which reappears in a broader context and interpretation in Beastly Tales From Here and There in **The Golden Gate**, the beats have dual purpose; firstly they symbolize the frustration of the main protagonist they are living with who in the humdrum of the cosmopolitan life of California are unable to their sexual urge, ironically due to lack of time because of which they have not been able to find the right companion. Hence the cats substitute the so- called mistress or master as the case may be, unless they find one Seth's animal have always contributed significantly to the theme of the novels.

The Fictional World of Vikram Seth: A Critique

Writers have perquisite to be nationalistic in theme if he or she so chooses, but to condemn a writer for being nationalistic is surely to miss the point. In case of Indian English writers Indian-ness is certainly not indispensable to their writing. Migrant Indian writers avoid the controversy due to their obvious and inarguable exposure to other cultures, but even in the case of those like, who were born in India and spent some of their formulate years here it cannot be held against then that key are not Indian, for with their transnational mobility, the culture they inherit is a global culture that includes India but is not limited to it. Seth in particular cannot be clubbed willy – nilly with the other Indo- Anglian writers because firstly, he was never overly nationalistic in his writing to begin with and secondly, for him India has not been the site for fashioning his identity as a writer, in these respects, as in several others, Seth is quite different from other Indian writers, for he demands no indulgence for being Indian and he does not pander to the west's current panchayat for lapping up Indian exotica. His work therefore cannot be evaluated on the basis of Indianess. In effect, Seth becomes confidently rooted in his footlessness, turning his iterant lifestyle into an asset rather than into a liability. His work, epitomes the integration of an individual sensibility with the ethos of global culture, Culture displacement cases to matter to Seth, as he assumes the role of the immigrant connoisseur who has mastered as a world alien to him on his own terms, effectively, colonizing the fictional space of the west. His writing stands in sharp contrast to the involutes style that other modern writers who wish to be taken seriously adhere to and which results from too much emphasis on stylistic devices. By his writing Seth has proved that it is not necessary to be obtuse in order to be appreciated.

The salient features of Seth's writing are that he is consistently true to the artistic process. Seth always tries to write as truly and literacy as he can and that no amount of persuasions from publishers to tailor bits of his work to suit a certain section would make him change it on estimated. Seth's literary achievement, it becomes evident that he cannot be compared to say a Rushdie or Naipaul for instance. This is because Seth's aspirations are very different. His desire as an author is never to be masterful, he has no designs on the reader, no accusations to hurl, no expectations that the reader should read more into his work than obvious if any motive at all is to be ascribed to his writing it would be the pleasure principle of art. The modernist de liking of what qualities as a literature with mainstream fiction as an abyss that Seth has adroitly bridged. By focusing on the simpler, universal passions, he addresses himself to readers irrespective of caste, creed or nationality and more importantly, his lucid style makes his work without feeding apprehensive about being subjected to the stylistic devices that often prove to be the bane of modern writing with its wit, humor and its keen sense of life there can no doubt that his work exhibits a timeless quality that assures Seth his place in posterity.

The name Vikram Seth conjures up the images of erudite cosmopolite, one who has baffled critics and readers alike as a writer who has unpredictable talents. He seems to be able to juggle words with consummate ease; his pen wields both poetry and prose with equal dexterity. He has made the English language his own and with his trademark transparent style, has gone a long way towards reinventing the contemporary literary scenes.

Seth is firm about his own priorities as an artist. He places clarity and intelligibility above verbal pyrotechnics. His writing is an embodiment of his intrinsic tolerance. But the 'piece de resistance' of Seth's style is his inimitable blending of what constitute the common man's bread with literary manna. Seth's gift is that that the combines the sensitivity of a poetic soul with the narrative dexterity a skill raconteur. Also, he has this in common with the great writes of all time, his themes poses substantial value a genuine human meaning, embracing life with all its passions, problems and vicissitudes. Seth's literary output is supported by this ample knowledge of life. The philosophy that Seth presents in his novels is fresh and serious and is expressed with sufficient power to provide more than superficial entertainment for the idler hour; his works poses a significance that no thoughtful reader is likely to overlook. This is evident because in discussing any of his works one finds oneself discussing life itself. All arts, dealing with man's actions in the world, become a criticism of life, and every author has values that may be inferred from his works. In the same way that Shakespeare's work, thought it has not been written with any express moral purpose in mind nevertheless presents a compendium of operations that can be categorized as general truths, Seth's writings too reveal his thoughts about life, his moral codes he has a holistic view of life, hope for a humane and harmonious world.

Seth's technique of writing has many singular features; some of these may be listed for a brief assessment. First of all, although he has a strong trend towards organizing his poetic pieces in a prose pattern of a song whenever the occasion comes. But whatever may be the rhythmic arrangement, there is invariably a mix of prose pattern which is often conversational and at times argumentative. At the same time it may be pointed out that his integration of prose and poetry is completely achieved, and the prose aspect adds a very pleasant dimension to the total aesthetic appeal of Seth's poems his fictional work in verse **The Golden Gate** where aspect of narration, observation and speculative ruminations mingle along with a mocking tone, in a structure impeccably organized to provide both the feel of prose and verse together, in an atmosphere which is both intimate and detached. In a different vein the words are used to pinpoint a context, a situation even a mod or an atmosphere.

The use of irony too, a part of total account, suggesting motivations and attitudes, both in short references as well as in larger contexts, is almost pervasive in Seth's writing. Even on many occasions the mix of humor and irony illuminating both the context and the point of view, has been deftly achieved. Seth not only chooses the Indian lexicons and characters for his an Indian tales but for the European and American backdrop too, succeeds in creating appropriate sensibilities. The central character in the Californian society in **The Golden Gate** is a solitary, melancholic character, much unlike the Indian protagonist in **A Suitable Boy** who are inextricably linked to the large community, the clan and the family tree they belong to Seth becomes a unique artist in the modern times whose versatility takes up back to the rich treasures of literature. Like literary giants Chaucer, Shakespeare and T.S. Eliot, Seth too has attempted translations of fables and also of some Chinese poetry without losing the regional thesaurus and flavor of original poetry.

Thus in Vikram Seth one fiends a multi- faceted personality, attempting a study of so many dimensions of literature is certainly an uphill task. Mere critical analyses of his arts cannot be enough, an in depth analysis of his art is possible only after keeping his usual life in perspective roughly in the five decades of the life spent at home and abroad. Moreover, an attempt to place Vikram Seth in the Indo- European tradition leads us to an in-depth study of the so called indo –Anglian writings too. The verse seems to how effortlessly whether it is description or conversation or even mental reflection; Seth harnesses the sonnet to fashion a tale that never lapses into boredom. Seth's diction is interspersed with Latin and French influences. Seth has been unjustly accused for not having found his voce and he counters with the facts that at different stages of his life and under the influence of different inspirations, he writes different things Seth says: "The wish to about is such a rare and mysterious feeling that it by notions of subject or geography or genre for good or ill, one must take one's visions as they came and be thankful for those that survive." (20)

Seth's work is characterized by disciplined form and context. It is also profoundly anti- romantic; the cheerful tenor of most of his books cannot quite displace the fact that his characters emerge from their various adventures with love and life as sadder and wiser creatures. Seth understands romance and impulse behind romantic or idealistic natures but disavows both for more level- headed and practical arrangement of affairs with gentle wit and wry humor Seth defuses romantic tendencies even in his own whitely self, and the result is that there is a quality of self- effacement in Seth's writings.

Vikram Seth is undeniably a writer among writers, someone who can be called the master craftsman of his generation. There is no doubt that with his technique both inherited and innovative and his refreshing attitude towards to creative process Seth has transformed the literary Ana and dazzled both the East and West as a writer with profound promise. He occupies a genre of his own, in final analysis; Seth is to his characters and the story, and the form. Everything else merely follows. He is a writer indisputably committed to his writing and the challenges involved therein: the development and fermentation in the academia leave him unmoved, and find little reflection in his works. Therefore it will be very interesting to calibrate the themes and techniques in the novels of Vikram Seth.

Refrences :-

1.   Guravi Gujrat, "The Astouding Success of Vikram Seth", Unsigned, 3 April 1993.

2.   Pawan K. Verma, " Of love, Loneliness and the Fine Art of storytelling" Hindustan times (Delhi) Sunday magazine May, 2, 1999.

3.   Ibid

4.   Ali Lakhani, "A Suitable Boy", (Review) Roungh, Vol 2, No 1 & 2, 1993: p57

5.   Michele Field, "Vikram Seth", Publishers Weekly, May 10, 1993: p46

6.   Dick Devis, "Byron Goes to San Francisco", Sunday Telagraph, June 29,1986

7.   Ibid

8.   Salman Rushdie, the Ground Beneath Her Feet Newyork: Henry Holt and Company 1999.

9.   Vikram Seth, An Equal Music (New Delhi Penguin 1999) p.3

10.   Shyam S Agrawalla, Vikram Seth's A Suitable Boy: search for an Indian Identity, New Delhi: Prestige Books, 1995: p28

11.   Maggie Gee "Double Helping Sef The Food of Love" Daily Telegraph, April, 3, 1999.

12. Rediff.coom   Interview   URL
www.rediff.com/chat/vikcha.html

13. Ibid, p-231

14. Vikram Seth, "writers on writing" Radio Series
Transcript. Australian Broadcasting Corporation
URL: http://www.abe.net.au/writers/writers
summary.

15. Jeremy Gavron, "A Suitable Boy" Daily Mail and
Gaurdian, July, 20, 1999.

16. "Introduction", The Poems 1981-1994, Penguin
India Ltd. 1995 pxv.

17. Makarand Paranjape, "A Conversation with Vikram
Seth, Mixed Beats and Cultural Products", Indian
Review of books (2)6, 1993: p20-24

18. Mappings, Culcutta Writers workshop, 1981: pix

19. From Heaven Lake, London: chatto and Windus,
1983 p178

20. Three Chinese poets, Faber and Faber Ltd, 1992:
pxvi

The Golden Gate – The Beginning of Narrative Technique

2.(A) Introduction of the Golden Gate

Vikram Seth is the master of art and narrative. He is an outstanding story – teller. Seth has an immense creative variety. He is a man of varied mood. His range of writing cannot be limited to one or two subjects. He combines various parts of the story skillfully. One part comes to another very naturally. Simplicity and vernacular use of language are among the factors which attract mostly in his narration. His description has pictorial quality. In his stories as well as in his novels, there are descriptions from common human life of market, journey, temple, music, party and from nature and weather like scenes of day break and evening. To write an epic - narrative on India, he chooses the conventional mode and style of the Victorians. He wrote an epical novel **"A Suitable Boy"**, on the vast Indian canvas while for presenting the ennui and loneliness of the American and European societies, he wrote medium sized novels using verse from and interior monologue respectively in *The Golden Gate* and *An Equal Music*. Verse form was used to show the fast life of the Californians, and for describing the dull lugubrious life of western musicians. He used an appropriate prose form „interior monologue". In his travelogue *from Heaven Lake*, he adopted vocative technique. This technique is varied and lucid. We find glimpse of all the aspects of life in Seth's writing. He shows pleasant and unpleasant, beautiful and abhorrent aspects of life. His novels are not only for entertainment, they have special art form. These novels are integrated in form and everything which is superfluous is carefully avoided. Seth uses unique language in his novels. All his works employ flawless English but with and Indian subject in *A Suitable Boy* he used translation of words with very local dialect. In this way, a witty narrative based on heightened passion displays Seth's unique hold on his subject and his medium.

Vikram Seth's first novel **The Golden Gate** is a novel, in the sense that this is a fiction in verse. Novel in verse is a thing of novelty. In the recent literary history, novels in verse have not appeared though Vikram Seth says he has drawn inspiration from Alexander Puskin who has composed *Eugene Onegin,* a novel in verse. Seth's The Golden Gate has all the ingredients to be described as an 'American novel'. It deals with the lifestyle, culture and love of present America. Regarding this Z.N.Patil in his article The image of America in Vikram Seth's **The Golden Gate** comments : "Some literary critics would like to classify Vikram Seth's **The Golden Gate**, a novel that breaks new ground in the sense that it is a novel written in sonnet form as an Indian novel in English just because of the reason that Vikram Seth was born in Calcutta and lived in India for about the first fifteen years of his life and he did not set foot in America until he attained the age of twenty three. But I personally feel that this alone is not enough to justify the novel as an Indo-English novel. 'Quite a few critics describe it as a California novel". (1)

C.N. Srinath in <u>Essays in Crtiticism,</u> comments: "Judging by his novel The Golden Gate, it is hard to see how Vikram Seth can be considered an Indian Writer except by accident of birth. There are few Indian references in the text, such as the "Taste of Honey" and the charioteer metaphor and the non-violent attitude of the peace marchers has obvious Gendlian connections... but there is nothing here that California has not possessed for a long time ....This is , in fact, a totally California novel"(2).

This is because of Seth's total involvement with life in California. Seth emphasizes that it is not his detachment but rather his love of California that is most valuable to him in writing the novel. Seth States that one cannot come with a cold and objective eye from outside and then write with affection about a place. One must have lived years in that place and not just observed for years. The novel is replete with enormous amount of information on California. The novel **The Golden Gate** is composed entirely in rhyming tetrameter sonnets. It consists of 594 sonnets, written in iambic tetrameter. And it follows the fourteen line stanza pattern of Eugene onegin. Regarding this, Seemita Mohanty in A Critical Analysis of Vikram Seth's Poetry and Fiction comments in the following way:

"Eugene onegin is written in verses of iambic tetrameter with the unusual rhyme scheme 'aBaBccDDeFFeGG' where the lowercase letters represent feminine rhymes and the uppercase represent masculine rhymes. This form has come to be known as the 'Onegin stanza'. Unlike the Shakespearian sonnet of 'abbacddceffegg' the Onegin stanza does not divide into smaller stanzas of four lines or two in an obvious way. There are many different ways the sonnet can be divided, for example the first four lines can form a quatrain or instead join with the 'cc' to form a sestet. The form's flexibility allows the author more scope to change how semantic sections are divided from sonnet to sonnet, while keeping the sense of unity provided by keeping a fixed rhyme scheme." (3)

2.(B) Writing Style of The Golden Gate

Vikram Seth's used this stanza in his novel *The Golden Gate.* Seth's rhyme scheme differs from traditional sonnet forms. The traditional sonnets were in pentameter, and the rhyme scheme employed were abba abba cde cde (Petrarchan) or ababbcbc cdcdsee (Spenserian) or abab cdcd efef gg

(Shakespearean). Seth's rhyme scheme is very much unlike these, and goes ababcdcd in octave and efefgg in sestet, and this is rare in the sonnet form.

Further, Seth interest in creative writing flourished when the sustaining support came from his friend and the writing mentor Timothy Steel who was a poet and teacher at the University of California. The collaboration between the two began in 1975, when the former was prevented from taking a creative writing course at Stanford University. Seth sought the help of his informal mentor, Timothy Steel. Gradually, the two grew so close that seth's first novel *The Golden Gate* was dedicated to Timothy Steel and a book of Timothy Steel's poems published by Random House was dedicated to Vikram Seth.

The Golden Gate amazed critics with its extraordinary form. Seth developed to remarkably readable effect, a satirical romance describing the lives and preoccupation of a group of young professionals in San Francisco. *The Golden Gate* proved to be another literary miracle by an Indian writer in English in the 1980s after Salman Rushdie's

Midnight Children. The focus of much critical attention has been the technical accomplishments of Vikram Seth in the writing of an entire novel in such a rigid and tightly controlled form, without allowing the contractedness of the sonnet to interfere with the easy pace of reading a contemporary light novel.

2.(C) Themes of The Golden Gate

The Golden Gate portrays San Francisco in its manifold charm the way Pushkin does for Russia. The breadth of the life is exhibited from its most trivial aspects to more contemporary, disputed and moral standards. Friendship, Love, work, play, sexuality, the nuclear age, single parent child rearing, death and the city are just some of the topics included. And there are the wonderful light touches of scrabble and chess, symphonies and art critics, interesting party scenes and personal resolution through advertisements. Such insignia's like the bumper stickers and billboard slogans seen while driving down a freeway are artfully and engagingly rendered in verse. If anything ties Seth's work together, it is the rootless, detached quality of the narrator. In **The Golden Gate,** however, Vikram

Seth's focus is on a very different world. Attention is directed towards what one reviewer refers to the ethos of the Yuppies of San Francisco. Located in the epicenter of the Andreas Fault, the inhabitants of San Francisco are constantly under the threat of physical destruction of earthquakes. Yet this is not only threat of Seth's protagonists. There are serious ruptures and cracks within the social fabric of the comfortable.

The term Yuppie is used to refer to the young people who come from across the world and work in Californian urban locality with high pay and high standard of living. The young people are very fond of fashionable life rather than traditional life, so they want to break some of their traditional knot and live according to their wish. These young people, who are settled in urban areas and have a good job, want to celebrate their life; hence they involve in current customary activities. Some people may lose their traditional and cultural roots because of their multi-cultural brought up. Thus knowingly or unknowingly the socio-culture of the young people is provided with modern needs. The young characters in the novel are the representatives of the twentieth century. They always involve in their official works, have all modern gadgets, and they proudly wear their official identity cards around their neck like a garland. Their food, culture, language, and living style reflect the modern society of California.

The yuppies' life has been generally analyzed by the demographic profile which reveals the psychological of the Yuppies and the reason behind their attitudes. Vikram Seth who authentically witnessed the lifestyle and socio-cultural status of the yuppies in the great city, San Francisco is able to produce a realistic portrayal of the socio- cultural life in America in the novel **The Golden Gate**. In this novel Vikram Seth touches all the possible concepts by his practical knowledge. He brings out the realistic picture of the Roman Catholic Church and its social activism along with the sufferings of gay people or bisexuals, and the struggle of craftsmen. He has clearly illustrated the American young people's life with their expectations, worries and success. The wonderful and realistic portrayals of the city of San Francisco make the readers see the far away region through the minds 'eye of the author: …

"…………… it
was not his detachment but
rather his love for California
that was the most valuable to
him in writing the book …
…..One can't come with a
cold and objective eye from
outside and then write with
affection about a place. One
must have lived in that place
and not just observed for
years." (4)

The Golden Gate is an in-depth exploration of society, specifically American society. Seth examines the fabric of American society, and pinpoints the factors that are tearing it apart. Critics deride the novel for being hedonistic but on a closer scrutiny it becomes clear that not only does the novel argue against a hedonistic lifestyle, it also manages to make good sense of the chaos that permeated every stratum of a fast paced culture, even suggesting remedial measures. The basic theme is of isolation and estrangement. Exploring the alienation in modern

American society, Trilling says, "…… the individual is not only isolated from society, he is isolated from every one he knows, even his own love partner". (5) Seth unflinchingly presents this malady afflicting modern society: the morbid preoccupation with one's own affairs to the exclusion of everything and everyone else, the selfishness inherent in the non-sharing of thoughts, time, and needs, the stubborn rejection of human bonding: in essence, the problem confronting modern urban society is that in it all the things that constitute the very structure of society have been torn down. In a quite manner, Seth strips the glamour from the American yuppiedom: there is more to this life than sunshine and California wine- there is loneliness so intense that people build walls around themselves to convince themselves that they are islands, there is self doubt, unrelenting professional pressure, no set of values to live by, confused moral codes, and ever increasing alienation from human touch.

Seth compels his characters to search for meaning in their lives, and to assume responsibility for their actions instead of blaming the world at large for everything that goes awry. There is little examination of the obscene amounts of money spent on defense outlays in the developed world, forcing the developing countries, with their impoverished populations, into untenable economic positions in the mindless and senseless race of nuclear proliferation. The novel presents the multicultural world through its eighteen century Russian antecedent and the twenty century cosmopolitan California. Seth likes to distance himself from the fashionable academic preoccupations. The novel is, in a sense, a literary curiosity. Not only does it unify poetry with fiction, it brings together a 19th century Russian antecedent with a modern American present. Seth describes in the most modern, the most sought after location of California that has come to represent, more or less, the aspiration of the Yuppies whose lives indeed substantiate the story, the novel spins an identifiable and popular yarn in old- fashioned metrical and rhymed verse. In this sense it bridges a chasm between the academic and the popular, giving vicarious satisfactions of both to each. Seth enters into the culture of his American world completely and is able to write about the lives of a specific class of Americans with great cultural interiority, making invisible his own Indian self. A borderless and multicultural world is conjured up by the novel and by the facts surrounding inspiration and its author. The author seems to be critiquing the hold of religious dogma, which twists natural sexual tendencies into something unnatural and deviant.

The Golden Gate, Seth's epic fiction in verse, borrows modernism's assumptions of ennui and purposelessness into the context of American upper middle class. The novel has been praised tor being able to "deconstruct the canonic models with a view to question, expose and dismantle the underlying structures and question the imperial assumptions." (6) such a critical ambition proves more than the efforts which this fiction actually allows. By adopting the sonnet form, Seth succeeds in showing the gap between romantic, courtly assumptions and culture behind the form against the dull, dry and highly practical life of the yuppies rather than "interrogate the socio-cultural assumptions entailed in the sonnet form." (7)

The novel portrays the socio-cultural life of California when the society has been gradually transformed as the hypermodern city. The ethos of the city has been changed due to the current trend and the people start to live their life according to the contemporary ethnicity. People give more importance to the social issues like housewarming ceremony, art exhibition and luxurious dinner. All the characters in the novel are associated with the above mentioned activities in one way or other way.

Vikram Seth portrays the cultural hybrid, restaurant culture, advertisement culture, music culture, art culture, ethnicity and nuclear weapon culture in this novel. Through these, the author brings out the contemporary issues which have been confronted by the young society. Both male and female become the victims of multiculture and cultural hibridity. A man who does not have a strong family or cultural background may not follow any particular rules and conventions. He may live according to his own wish but is not able to mingle with the society. Vikram Seth highlights the issues in the middle class family which includes divorce, unemployment, loneliness, and frustration caused by cross-culture.

Seth has made every effort to portray an intimate Californian lifestyle. He has said that it was not his detachment but rather his love for California that was the most valuable to him in writing the book. One cannot come with a cold and objective eye from outside and write with affection about a place. One must have lived years in that place and not just observed for years. There are a number of details that range from the seemingly inconsequential to more serious social issues open to debate such as housewarming parties, winemaking picnics, weekend jaunts followed by sumptuous breakfasts and gestalt group parties.

The Golden Gate depicts different types of love among people discussed in this novel through romantic love is in focus. There are three key pairs in this work: John and Liz, Phil and Claire, Art and Sue. It is also known that Phil and Ed are also in homosexual affair for a brief period and John and Janet Hayakawa are also erstwhile lovers and present friends.

The key character is John whose acquaintances fill out the multitude of San Francisco. The novel begins and ends with him. He is a blond haired, good –looking, healthy, employed, ambitious, sound, solvent, self-made, self possessed but a depressed person. John is a young man of twenty six and is described as aloof, prim and lonely. He longs for a family which he thinks will cushion his solitude. John feels a cold cast of self-pity envelops him. He has no family to care for him. His mother is dead and his English father after his retirement from government service dwelling in his native Kent rarely responds to the letters sent by John. When John blames his father for not promptly and frequently responding to his letter, his father camouflages himself behind the poor service of postal department. If he is in touch with his son who suffers a sense of loneliness, it might comfort John to some extent. After he leaves the college, his life has grown duller and more monotonous. Even though he leads an economically and financially comfortable life, he has nobody with whom he can have sharing of things. After the completion of his education, he does not show much interest in keeping his friendship with friends intact. He prioritises his professional life over his friendship. He works with the nuclear firm which manufactures nuclear arms. Loneliness may have frustrated him to great extent but it has not made him unempathetic. Whenever his co-workers are in trouble, he makes it a point to lend them a helping hand to come out of it. When a fellow worker of John is fired from his job, John takes up the case with the boss who is very stubborn and obstinate and says what is done is done and he cannot do anything about it.

A fellow engineer's been fired

John pleads his cause (what is done is done his boss replies). (8)

John with his perseverance champions the cause of his dismissed colleague and he emerges successful in reinstating him. This is an instance that shows the empathy of John for others. That he shares the grief and sorrow of his friends becomes obvious and evident from this incident. But at the same time he has undergone a transformation in him. His friends say he is not what he used to be. Work and the syndrome of possessions leave little time for life's digression. And it cannot be said that his present plight is due to his employment with the defense but his childhood brought up and upbringing also has impacted him to a great extent. In his childhood, he is not able to enjoy motherly love, affection and care. It may also be a reason why he has completely confined to his work and not moving with others freely. After he returns home from the office, to get rid of the pain of loneliness, he endeavors' hard to do his reading but he finds himself unable to do it due to lack of concentration.

He suffers the pain of loneliness and in order to overcome it, he visits ice-cream parlors where the sight of girls being together and their conversation among themselves remind him about his solitude. Such scene sitting and chatting together further worsens his plight and he leaves the place at once. On an occasion returning home, he thinks back to his college days and his college friends such as Phil and others and the nights they spent together. That he suffers emptiness in his private life which is so frustrating that it forces him to make calls to his friends such as Phil over phone. On second thoughts, he gives up that idea since Phil has committed himself to nuclear disarmament. John works with Lungless Lab where nuclear – weapons are manufactured and he is afraid that their relationship, if renewed, will be politicized. Then John makes a call to Janet Hayakawa who is of Japanese nationality and erstwhile lover and present friend of John.

John falls in love firstly with Janet Hayakawa and later this relationship falls apart. But John and Janet continue their relationship as friend. Janet always thinks about John and his solitude. She wants to relieve him of that. So that she takes an action and give a newspaper advertisement for a girl friend or spouse for John. At the advertisement of Janet three girls respond positively. The two girls Wasp Bluestocking and Belinda Beale fail in their attempt to impress John. Liz Dorati is a twenty seven year old, high-powered ex-Stanford Law school attorney. She is beautiful, vivacious, blue-eyed, well –rounded blonde who is from a family of Italian immigrant wine-growers. John is impressed by her handwritten reply that Jane forwards to him, and invites her to meet him. They share a passionate whirlwind romance that lasts for a brief period. It is also known that when people are used to complimenting her elegance and prettiness, she silently accepts it without responding to them. And Liz' mother Mrs. Dorati in the strongest terms advises her to get married. Liz manages her saying that after her studies get over and she obtains a law degree, she will enter into wedlock.

John is seen meeting her during day time because his earlier attempts in romance prove to be a fiasco as he meets them at night. John and Liz meet at a restaurant called Cafe Trieste. When the meeting takes place there, Janet Hayakawa who is instrumental in making this arrangement because of her care and concern for John turns up and seeing them talking so closely to each other, leaves unwilling to disturb them. John's intimate conversation with Liz delights Jane to a great extent. She being his former lover and present well wisher and friend is quite delightful to see John forgetting about all his worries immersing himself in conversation with Liz. Unable to Part Company,

Than John and Liz move towards another restaurant called Tree of Heaven. During their talk, Liz mentions her pet cat Charlemagne to him. Since John has so far suffered only solitude and loneliness in his life, his new relationship and affair with Liz is really God sent to him. During his childhood also, John has not been blessed with motherly love and affection. On an occasion Phil states to Liz John's odd and strange behavior can be attributed to his lack of caring and affectionate upbringing. Considering all these factors, John's affair with Liz means so much to him and is of paramount importance in terms of love life of John. After Janet Hayakawa, only now John has managed to earn the heart of a young girl. That he is very happy is a surprise to John who states to Liz about it. Liz asks him why he is surprised to be happy and if he gets downcast often. Liz is delighted to comfort him.

Seth also takes a close look at the institution of marriage. The ideal marriages presented in the novel are those of Janet's parents and Liz's parents. Both these marriages are based on old values, with both spouses committed to one another and to their respective families. In stark Contrast is the marriage of Phil with Claire and the relationship between John and Liz. Both these associations falter because they have been made by people who are too self-involved to try to change themselves for someone else. On the other hand, Phil and Liz succeed in maintaining a relationship chiefly because they have learnt a lesson from their previous relationships. Seth also advocates that shared likes and dislikes and compatible interests, not mere physical attraction, are the foundations of a long term relationship. Liz ultimately recognizes this and it is for this reason that she chooses the dull but sensible Phil over the passionate but volatile John and Seth seems to commend her choice.

Another theme in the novel is that of nuclear warfare. Seth expatiates upon the theme unhurriedly, using narration, description, dialogue, sermon, demonstration, and peace marches diatribe, to get the point across. Nuclear insanity is a very contemporary theme and it is very significant in this novel because both the theme and the novel are so quintessentially American. America is one of the few countries where people are aware enough to protest the acquisition of nuclear weapons. In addition to this, how other things also bring about their separation and split is analyzed. John finds himself in a situation where he feels that Charlemagne, Liz's interest in tuneless songs, her tofu-eating and Kefirdrinking habits further aggrieve him. Liz's caring, affectionate and loving enquiries which once delight him now do not give him any joy any more. He realizes that his love for Liz does not get bright. On an occasion, mulling over the cat, and Liz's defense of it, he comes out of the room and happens to meet Phil coming in a car.

While both friends meet, Phil realizing the dullness and grief of John asks him about the reason of it. John, in a dull voice replies that Liz loves Charlemagne more than she loves him. He cites Liz's abundant affection for the cat as the reason for his grief. Phil pacifies John saying that Liz is not dizzy in her affection. John asks him not to defend her. Phil comes out saying that he does not take any side and he urges John to speak his mind to his friend. At this point, John mentions that he never thinks a cat wreck his joy and peace. Phil attempts to offer comfort to him. In due course of their talk, John sees that the left eye of Phil is damaged and he enquires about it. He further questions whether it has been caused by a lover and Phil answers that it happened last week.

John who is very traditional and orthodox in matters related to sex is really shell shocked to hear it from his friend. It is very hard to digest for him. And he shouts to Phil that he needs brain – transplantation. Flying into rage, John asks him how Phil, a married man, can do such things. To another question from John as to what two men can do together, Phil replies he can try it himself to know more about it. That Phil has homo-sexual relationship with Ed is an unbearable and intolerable shock to John. Both have become uncomfortable and incompatible in the presence of each other. In matters with regard to Love and Romance, they are poles apart. They are staring at each other.

John, at the start of the novel, is portrayed as a lonely and solitary person. He has to live continuously with his loneliness. Janet the only well wisher for John died in an accident at the end of the novel. John's love life is a total failure and has no family member also. His mother is no more and his father after his retirement from government and dwelling in his native counters rarely responds to the letters sent by John. Loneliness may have frustrated him to great extent but it has not made his unempathetic. Whenever his co- workers are in trouble, he helps them.

Another dominant theme in the novel is that of homosexuality, which makes the novel particularly true to the American way of life. Homosexuality is by no means an American invention but due to its prevalence in American society it has acquired almost a cult status there. But *The Golden Gate* is not an attempt to glorify homosexuality. It is true that it is Phil, a homosexual, who is rewarded with a rich family life at the end of the novel, while John has nothing left but the memories. Seth espouses the superiority of personal judgment over any opinions held by conventions. It is a credit to Seth's art that the novel does not glorify homosexuality, nor does it degenerates into a vicious diatribe against it. One of the few Indian writers who deal with the issue of homosexuality, Seth has also spearheaded a campaign in India recently in connection with it being a legal offensive here. While Seth portrays his two homosexual characters with a great deal of sympathy, yet aware that it is not a socially accepted mode of sexuality. When Ed and Phil first make love, the narrator anticipates and critiques the official censor comparing him to an insensitive swine, which point to an understanding that homosexual passion is not wrong; on the contrary it is entirely natural. However censoring it and pushing it behind the closer is definitely questionable. These seem to be the views of the narrator and the Phil, and the authorial stand projected in the novel. The homosexual relationship between Phil and Ed is a thematic concern, but homosexuality as an issue; does not contribute to the central tension of the narrative, nor is Seth concerned with its etiology. Contemporary queer theories explore heterosexual norms that pervade society and examine how these are shaped by society's regulatory discursive practices. While Seth speculates on varied sexual preferences, he retains his legible relation with heterosexual readership. Phil's encounter into homosexuality is very brief. His sexual identity is molded by circumstances. Phil's desire for Ed is replaced by his relationship with Liz. He eventually marries Liz and both fulfill their social obligation of propagation. The norm is thus restored when the couple gives birth to the mandatory grandson. Seth reverts to gender roles as they are created in relation to the social institution of marriage and family, and which conventionally involves both sexes. Twenty three-year old Edward Dorati, who as we have seen as the younger brother of Liz, is a homosexual, is caught in a dilemma.

Nature and the landscape are another themes of *The Golden Gate*. The landscape is always there in the novel, now smiling, berating, outstretching and dwarfing the human played out. In the novel both the love in the air and loss in the mind are portrayed movingly and vividly in furthering the storyline. Nature also receives her due share of attention in the novel. Nature is an inseparable part of the world Seth's characters inhabit and impress herself upon their almost compellingly. Seth does not use nature to contrast the beauty and simplicity of the Natural world with the sordidness and complexity of human life, but to the characters in the novel, the apprehension of the natural phenomenon brings them a serenity that is absent in their lives. It is for this reason that Janet, in spite of busy life she leads, goes to the bay to watch the whales migrate south for the winter, John, though cynical and worldly-wise, and is not immune to the beauty of the hills. Seth describes the natural beauty of the Bay Area, as opposed to the artificiality of a life controlled by technology. A marvel of engineering skill in steel, The Golden Gate Bridge is a suspension bridge that carries its burden with no visible means of support. Within the text, the bridge functions as more than just a connector between two geographical locations in the Bay area. Rather it enables the protagonists to connect back with their natural surroundings, and then with each other. Ed drives across the "tall-spanned bridge after an argument with Phil. And as he surveys the city from the bridge, "a benediction'" steals over his heart, and he decides to write to Phil. After Phil has a bitter argument with John, he and Liz take a drive together to the Bay, and walk across the bridge: "The most majestic spun by man- whose threads of steel through mists and showers, Wind, spray, and the momentous roar of ocean storms, link shore to shore" (9) While on the bridge, Phil and Liz open out to each other about their difficult relationships with Ed and John respectively.

One basic theme is that of isolation and estrangement, exploring the alienation in modern American society. Trilling says, 'Seth unflinchingly presents this malady afflicting modern society: the morbid preoccupation with one's own affairs to the exclusion of everything and everyone else, the selfishness inherent in the non-sharing of thoughts, times, and needs, the stubborn rejection of human bonding: in essence, the problem confronting modern urban society is that in it all the things that constitute the very structure of society have been turn down'. Most American men and women are unwilling to sacrifice what they perceive as their freedom, by committing to a permanent relationship. This fanatic obsession for keeping the heart aloof from rest of the body lies at the root of the problem. In psychological terms this is known as 'relationship anxiety'- the refusal to grow into a mature relationship. Almost every major character in the novel suffers from this anxiety and John most of them all. However Ed's anxiety is of a different kind; he wants the heart without the body to keep his soul guiltless. But does not want to face the fact that this is not what he really wants.

The theme of the novel is one of the classic materials of all comedy- man's search and the various mishaps that befall him in the course of that search, although the rest of the novel leads less in the traditional comic ending, than surprising. John Brown, the central character of this novel, is a Silicon Valley computer professional who's highly successful career stands in abysmal contrast to his personal life, which lives much to be desired. John is an emotional entity. Nobody wants him beyond his work, and this irks him no end. Beneath all his trivalent capers and his outward aggressiveness, he has all the basic human need to be loved by somebody. His only female friend is Janet Hawakaya, erstwhile lover, now, through mutual agreement, the two shares the friendship that is shielded from all passion.

Morality is a major theme of the novel. Seth does not subscribe to the concept of conventional Indian morality. As an artist, he recognizes the complexities of human nature, unpalatable though they may be. The moral code present in the novel is the moral code that America lives by: casual sex is a way of life, as are homosexual relationships, picks- up bars and so –on. Social morality, or what one owes to the world at large, has been brought to forefront by the episode of the peaceful demonstration against Lungless Labs. Seth unambiguously says that one must look beyond one's personal world to what one can do for society. John obviously is a loser, dejected and desolate. He feels insulted. He feels his virility has been undermined. He is unable to comprehend the reason of his rejection by Liz. In order to compensate for his virility, he starts visiting bars. His involvement with those bar girls gives him a sadistic pleasure. Seth, the patient moral teacher, gives John another chance to revive his love relation with Janet who had ignited six years backing Janet's heart. After seeing John in lust, Janet endeavors to alleviate his sufferings by giving him company. Janet is still afraid of expressing her love to him, while John is embittered with the World is unable to comprehend his love for her. Janet being a good human being and a considerable friend feels it is her duty to unite Liz, and Phil with their estranged friend, John. She throws a party at her home and invites everyone, all her friends, Phil Liz and John. But unfortunately, Janet never succeeds in her plan; her plan dies with her when she together with Matt and his family members meets a fatal accident, Only their son Chuck and the driver survive the accident. However, quite ironically Janet, though dead, accomplishes what she could not do while living. Seth undoubtedly gives a very poignant turn to the novel but a rich and powerful one. Her absence once again leaves John forlorn and distressed. But, there is a difference in this reaction.

John is not retaliatory but guilty that he never expressed his love for her. He realizes that she loved him undeludedly, unconditionally, asking for nothing in return. Janet becomes richer as she is able to reunite the three friends. She becomes richer ironically for the press too which had always evaded her and her music. It reports the news of her death as 'Young Artist Mowed Down in Her Glory'. They even pester her parents to reveal 'Relics' of their distinguished daughter. Janet's work of art is referred to as relies i.e. possession of a holy person that is deemed fit to be treasured alter one's death. Generally speaking, a good, virtuous character's goodness is not recognized in his life time, and on realization people make him immortal. Hence, a good person is remembered for his deeds and inevitably his soul becomes immortal. Besides, Janet's death has a cathartic effect on John, it takes him realize his flaw. A complex web of sense and sensibility on various levels are erected, making it an extremely sophisticated parody. Seth rejects the European generic form, replacing it with tetrameter versification. This enables him to interrogate the socio-cultural assumption entailed in the sonnet form. At the same time this brilliant post- modernistic oeuvre puts him firmly in the league of great Augustan Satirists. The novel ends satisfactorily. A healthy nine pound baby is born to Liz and Phil. A large-hearted and compassionate couple that they are, they accommodate willingly Matt and Joan s son Chuck, Paul (Phil's son), Janet's Cuff and Link, and Liz's Charlemagne. Having overcome is timidness, Ed is adamant on standing on his own feet. Interestingly, the baby is as healthy as the fertile, complete family of Phil and Liz. Both suggest to John that he should be their son's godfather and the name baby 'John. The novel ends at a positive note. John decides to pay his heart's arrears by resuming friendship with the two. Seth contrives an end to the story that is traditional, combining the beliefs of all great thinkers and writer; Indian or Western. He seems to say 'As you sow so you reap'. John errs like other characters but refuses to learn from his mistake.

Family is another dominant theme in the novel **The Golden Gate**. There are several studies which offer excellent analyses of Seth's commitment to the family as a social unit: this aspect runs through all his novels, and predominantly affects the choices his heroines make in both *The Suitable Boy* and *An Equal Music*. Seth presents before us the two kinds of families in this novel. One is the traditional biological family such as the Doratis, held together by strong ties of love strengthened by their close bonding with nature. Michael Dorati is a farmer. His wife yearns that the children should marry and add to the family. Their lives are tied to the pastoral cycle of growth and regeneration. The other kind of family is engendered through the ties of friendship. The brotherhood enjoyed by Phil and his circle of friends-Mrs. Craven and her daughter, Matt and Joan Lammount who are killed, and others would fall under this category. This kind of family is seen as a product of the modern situation of fragmented social units in metropolises. Such a family is diffuse, but its members still enjoy the social anchoring made possible by the family unit. The activities at the Dorati vineyard and the wine pressing are similar to the olive picking and picking at Phil's chuck is adopted by Phil, a friend of his father's, and Mrs. Craven provides the mothering to both Chuck and Paul. By extension, Phil and his campaigners conceive of humanity as the great human family and their campaign is to save it from nuclear catastrophe. If the inescapable loneliness of the individual in the contemporary metropolitan world is symbolized by

John, Phil stands for the humanistic conception of the community as family. In the final analysis, the live characters are either handed gifts of spouse, children, pets, and togetherness or are left lonely and unloved, according to the degree of their fidelity to the family values, their adaptability and their ability to tale on responsibility for themselves and others. Phil and Liz come out as winners; in their marriage the two different kinds of families too come together, and this is spelt out clearly in the mixed brood they inherit. Poor Janet is killed; John, obscurant as he is, could only be taught by death. But some redemption is possible for John even as he grieves, there is the knowledge of Janet's love that sustains him, the friendship extended by Phil and Liz and the prospect of being godfather to their baby. Babies and children are important to Seth as his other novels reveal, and he rewards his errant character with some association with one. The family then is important, but families, important as they are, can be sometimes deeply suffocating and full of human fallibilities at close quarters: possessiveness, meanness, hard heartedness, the list is endless. His partiality for the family is a part of these concerns.

A theme can be successfully and powerfully displayed only with the help of techniques. Yes, it is the various implements and tools which enable the writer to express his thoughts and convey his emotions effectively and according to his expectations. As regards its form, it seems to be the outcome of a judicious choice. As a novel of plot and character, **The Golden Gate** is very thin indeed, in essence being little more than a succession of musical beds. Seth gets so used to his writing in this form that even the acknowledgement, the dedication, and the table of contents have been versified. The opening line is arresting for its humorous dig at the lengthy epic style. The novel is a formal type of poetry with modern moral and spiritual dilemmas. The sonnet form is harnessed by Seth in a manner that it oscillates from being merely functional in taking the story forward to being rich in poetic eloquence. In the novel, Seth uses the broader base of fiction to unite the two genres of fiction and poetry. Realizing the advantages verse wields over prose, Seth uses it to communicate his experiences effectively.

Seth's novel presents a very unique combination of the sentimental with the mock-heroic. A mock-heroic work is defined as a type or Satirical verse that presents comically trivial matters in a heroic and epic manner. Seth, who has stated that **The Golden Gate** is somewhat mock- heroic in some of its aspects, is quick to point out that, though his characters are there only to make fun of or as playthings of his whimsical imagination but it has tragedy too. Also it doesn't use iambic pentameter, which is the standard mock-heroic meter, but iambic tetrameter.

The Bible is a third recurring reference in *The Golden Gate*. *The Bible* represents in the novel an older set of moral beliefs from which most of the fictional characters in the novel are alienated when LIZ and John make love it is said: "The loving pair has bit the apple of mortal knowledge." (10) Ed, rejecting Phil's homosexual advances says: "The Bible says' if a man lies, with a man, he must surely die." (11) Father O' Hare delivers an anti-nuclear speech: "By Christ's own sacrifice and passion/we cannot finch". (12) The Bible like *The Golden Gate* represents a permanent cultural influence on Western Civilization, permeating the modern world, questioning it and gelatinizing it for the reader. As Linda Hutcheon tells us: "No text is without its inter-texts" (13) Seth deliberately plays up references to other texts to merge the world of other texts into the discourse of his work and to make them a part of its identity. Various authors are mentioned in passing in the novel- Dostoevsky, Mann, Bede, John takes Belinda Beale to see William's Cat on a Hot Tin Roof, and the troubled, steamy passions portrayed in that play lend and intensity to the experience of the Californian characters.

The Golden Gate concerns itself with characters exploring versions of and discovering illusions and exploring other realities. Also, in the novel minor characters become major characters and major characters are relegated to the background in the novel. Thus, the number of references to other texts in Seth's novel testifies to the fact that literary works are enriched by other literary works and in the postmodern era this factor is celebrated, not played down, by the writer. The intertextuality of *The*

Golden Gate places the discourse of the novel in broader framework, opposing and questioning its particular grounding m a specific socio- historic Context. Seth's energies clearly were channeled into his poetic craft, which is one of the most superior kinds. A verse novelist faces the twin demands of narrative and versification; both have to work if the work has to succeed as novel and as poetry; Character, plot, metre and rhyme all demand the novelist's attention. His verse draws its style from conversation and manages different kinds of speech registers with ease and aplomb: short interjections, pithy reflections, jokes and jargon- it contains all. In his sonnets, syntactical endings do not always coincide with line endings, and nor, sometimes, with the end of the sonnet, running over into the next poem giving the work the racy quality of a novel. Seth uses multiple registers of discourse: the pedantic verbosity of academics and critics, the flippant conversation between friends, the lingo of executives and the rhetoric political speeches, all attribute to the pace of narrative. His verse remains on the surface and there is effortless profundity in his poetry. He makes his verse speak the spirit of the society he represents and the brilliance of his verse and its speed reflect the brittleness of the fast paced lives he speaks for.

The Golden Gate is an artistic and narrative triumph. The novel in verse is a veriable feast in which Seth serves equally appetizing humour and sadness. The coruscating language of Seth's crisp narrative combines vitriolic polemic with some squelchy sentimentality and a soft, downy sensuality. One of the most sustained pieces of serious, even sententious writing in *The Golden Gate* is Father O Hara's speech in the Chapter 7.16-7.34. He thematizes war, disarmament, peace and civil liberty, and very unlike anything else in *The Golden Gate*, Using several descriptions that qualify as the grotesque, Seth here critiques the greatest killing machine that human beings have ever invented: war and, its newest toy, the nuclear bomb. In one particularly ferocious passage at careens and ricochets between abrasive polemic and polite humanism. Seth condemns all polities as anti-human. There are many other passages in the middle of the love story which are in themselves interesting *The Golden Gate* is a remarkable Verse Novel that made readers spellbound across the globe for the obvious novelty depicted in the combination of two genre- novel and poetry. The novel traces the trials and tribulations of John as he comes to terms with his own loneliness and the sexual aberrations of his friends and acquaintances. True to the tradition of a Verse Novel, it fulfills the criteria of a novel in thirteen chapters that deals with the contemporary world of California, which comprises neither mythical nor heroic but ordinary human beings, fraught with human frailties. The demand on a 'Naturalist Writer is to depict life completely and objective honesty, to show things as they really are. John in *The Golden Gate* is a naturalist hero as Seth gives a true documentation of his life with objective honesty. Seth reveals great dexterity at conveying the anxiety, trepidations, pleasure and pain through appropriate imagery and rhythm. Only a gifted poet could have done justice to it with such ingenuity and skill. Seth chooses the sequence for his novel to describe California and its people. In the novel he has depicted a range of loves which are possible and acceptable in a 'modern' "metropolis" evincing unique culture.

Through the elements of post modernism in Seth's work, Seth is known as a post modernistic novelist. ***The Golden Gate*** is a psychological profile. It describes a set of behavioural and psychographic attributes that have come to constitute a commonly believed stereotype. Yuppies' traditional trends in which their parents stood for traditional aesthetic values and post modern trends in which they are the worshippers of money will present a very interesting reading. Seth is one of the successful challengers of prevailing literary tradition. Interestingly enough tradition itself is used as a moral method to challenge tradition. He uses the broader base of novel merely as a stepping stone to unite the two genres of novel and poetry. There is innovation in the tradition, stanzaic sonnet form for fiction. He presents imaginative and creative union of two genres. He contributes to the blurring of genre theory one of the controversial obsession of post modernism.

Post modernism is generally referred to the changes and the developments that came since 1940's. Post modernism is reaction against traditional form. Seth chooses a technique that would most suit his subject. He defines John as a naturalist hero and deals with his existentialism. Seth takes up the verse form that Pushkin has used for his novel. He nevertheless evinces an eclectic taste for varied forms which dealt in other chapters but deliberately discards parody, magic realism or science fiction form being used by his contemporaries Rushdie, Amitabh Ghosh, Allen Seally and others. Seth's predilection is ultimately for consolidation of the relationship. He reveals with under- current of humour and irony. ***The Golden Gate*** is privileged as post modernism fiction through its form of tour de force, Instead of lush grew meadows, the trees and daffodils pervading the poetry of romantics, these poets brought in dirt squalor and nasty smell of modern life. It was known as post modernistic poetry.

Seth uses Google, nuclear, software, engineer, Bomb, love and break up as elements of post modernism which remains in California society in ***The Golden Gate.*** This novel appears to remain a testament to the modernist sentiments which stress the predominance of valueless relationship. John in the searching of spouse or sibling wanders alone here and there and in parlours, points to the meaninglessness of contemporary existence of modern American society. All settings of American culture, it makes easy to say Vikram Seth is as a post modernism writer of fiction after 1990s.

Vikram Seth is a writer of Post-modern age and as such there are elements of postmodernism in his work. He is a genius writer. History of every literature is a witness to the fact that rebellion always resurrects itself in every age and every country. The rebellion rises phoenix like-from the ashes mundane to manifest itself in all fine arts including literature. In fact that rebellion manifests itself particularly in his first novel. **The Golden Gate** is a prime illustration of subversive rebellion in Indian English Fiction of the Nineteen Ninetees. Though "Professor, Publisher and critic each voiced their doubts". He is infact one of the successful challengers of prevailing literary tradition. Interestingly enough tradition itself is used as a model method to challenge tradition. Inform, he uses the broader base of novel merely as a stepping stone to unite the two genres of novel and poetry.

Vikram Seth is a puissant promoter of postmodernism. He has a rather unnerving experience because he carries his subversive rebellion to nearly every aspect of his book. In terms of plot it is unexpected in the norm. The trials, tribulations, agonies and mental terminations of John as he comes to terms with his beloved Liz marrying his best friend Phil, who has had a homosexual affair with his future wife's younger brother Ed, are the most unusual twist and unexpected turns of the story. The novel therefore resists narrative closure in the best Post-modernist tradition.

After the writer throws light on 'love' portrayed in the novel, he deals with depiction of 'life' in San Francisco. Before that, the book makes an observation that it is disheartening to note that the end of the novel ends the lives of loving hearts such as Janet Hayakawa, Mrs. Dorati and Matt Lamont and his wife. When Janet Hayakawa has arranged a party to celebrate the success of her sculptural works, she has scheduled it at the venue, 'Marcus Laded'. She has invited Phil and his pregnant wife Liz, John and others as well. When she picks up Matt Lamont and his wife in person in her car to bring them to the party, the car is involved in a deadly accident which cost their lives, except the kid Lamont. The doctor couple also has been of great help him to Phil's family. They planned to spend their latter part of lives for the wild life protection. In Vikram Seth, the Literary Genius: An introduction, by Pramod K. Nayar, it is thus described with regard to the story of *The Golden Gate*:

"*The Golden Gate* is ultimately a sad love story. All the requisite elements are present: the search for love, first love, circumspect first moves, gradual acceptance of the indispensability of the loved one, the move towards sharing a life and space, the consequent anxieties and adjustments the "betrayal", the turn to heartbreak and the death of the loved one. John's search for love, his relationship with Liz the break-up the entry of Phil as the sympathetic friend during the moment of crisis and the unfortunate death of Janet just when John appears to be finding himself again- all narrated with a touch of sardonic humour that translucently reveals the underlying theme of the book. This theme is to be

Seth's staple in each of his three novels: the search for love or at least companionship by alienated, intelligent and sensitive individuals indeed **The Golden Gate** might very well be called a sentimental novel"(14).

Seth's impressive and absolutely justifiable speech assumes much more significance and importance in the context of worldwide opposition against weapons of mass destruction. Only on this occasion when Phil's presence as well as his action is solid, Liz turns up there to express solidarity with their cause. While asked to deliver a speech, she states that on account of their follies humans can have for their sufferings and agonies in the event of nuclear war. How it can be defended when massive devastation and destruction is inflicted on the planet and its flora and fauna. This incident has cemented their affair further. With regard to the speech delivered by Father O Hare Pramod K. Nayar and R.K. Dhavan in a Paper entitled Vikram Seth, the Literary Genius: An Introduction collectively published their comments in the following manner :

"One of the most sustained pieces of serious even sententious writing in **The Golden Gate** is Father O'Hare's Speech. His speech thematises war, disarmament, peace and civil liberty and is very unlike anything else in *The Golden Gate*. However, when we look at the sensitivity of individuals in Seth's **An Equal Music** and the descriptions of communal unrest and politics in *A suitable Boy*, one realizes that these passages are only prolepsis. Using several descriptions that qualify as the grotesque, Seth here critiques the greatest killing machine that human beings have ever invented! War and its newest try, the nuclear bomb." (15)

The enjambment, the "continuation of a sentence without a pause beyond the end of a line, couplet or stanza," is used to create meaningful effects, and also used to move the narrative action forward in a prosaic manner. (16) Third, we consider rhythm, both the actual 'timed' rate of flow of the words or motion, and the precise depression level in the wave pattern created. As in song, downbeat is an element of this, as well as meter, usually treated separately. Conversational style in **The Golden Gate** is much informed by this aspect, varying for the different characters, as well as for the author's own remarks to the 'Reader.' Fourth, we consider melody: here, the musical effect of the sonnet, passage, or sequence is noted. Is it monotonous or not? Hymn-like, psalm-like, prayer-like, a folk-song? What is the character of its musical effect? We see this of note, particularly, in the more culturally and religiously-based dialogues of Seth's <u>Golden Gate</u> characters, as well as in a broader dialogic sense, according to the theme of note. Fifth, we note the significance of harmony, the degree to which the verse elements are harmoniously constructed in their variations from and similarities to each other. This includes examining points at which they are intentionally rendered in a disharmonious manner, and why.

"Imagery is both a literary effect and an organizing principle of separate note. This term encompasses both textual effects that elicit visual images, or "mental pictures," and, more broadly, "figurative language" used as "vehicles" for metaphors and similes." (17) Here, we are interested in whether the verse is intentionally designed to

elicit, refer to, or explain visual images, as well as enhance other understandings of the text. (18) For example, The Golden Gate includes landscapes and nature's beauty, described with stylistic precision, an effect obtained by using specific familiar lyrical phrasings (19) with certain textual elements. In other examples, nature is a background for a scene linked to characters' thoughts and their personal development; while imagery which introduces us to artists' art sculptures, in particular, invites amusing interpretations, as artistic creations are 'seen' by an artist, her friends, and her critics, and then also by the reader through Seth's words.

Much of **The Golden Gate's** narrative is pushed forward by dialogue. This includes dialogue between the characters, internal dialogue in characters' thoughts, and the shared dialogue of the author with the reader. Dialogue occurs by phone, on walks, in cafes, restaurants and bars, at parties and at home. An explication of some of these illustrates how meaning and direction are created in poetic conversation, how the narrative action is pushed forward, and the ways that stylistic devices inform our understanding of the relationships and concerns of the characters. Let us look at some examples.

The thematic revolt is also worth noting, it traces the bitter expierences of the hero, John Brown as he comes to terms with his own loneliness and the sexual aberration of his friends and acquaintances. It can be considered as a "buildingsroman" or a novel dealing with the coming of age of the protagonist. It is the first English novel to deal with homosexuality in an open, frank, candid and bold manner, revealing all the aspects connected to it emotional, religious, physical, sexual, emotional and psychological. In this respect, the novel proves to be metafictation as the novelist writes about the writing of the written. He is also indicative of the authorial involvement with the readers and the text as opposed to the earlier trends. Stylistically, speaking Vikram Seth is a very conscious craftsman with a purpose. He invokes muse and subverts the social political, religious, literary and cultural myths. Thereby deconstructing and dismantling the underling traditional assumptions. He also makes the European generic form the target of his parody. This provides him the pretext to interrogate the socio-cultural political assumptions in the sonnet form. He deconstructs the canonical models with the view to question, expose and dismantle the underlying structures and questions the imperialist assumptions.

2.(D) Reviews of The Golden Gate

Reviewing and rewriting the mythic structure and assumptions are therefore Vikram Seth's greatest contribution to the new discourse in Indian English Literature. In reality the publication of Vikram Seth's ***The Golden Gate (1986)*** is a milestone in the postmodern era of Indian English fiction. It is hailed rightly for its technical excellence as after a period of 150 years a novel is written in verse. Probably it is the first English novel written in verse. There are large numbers of postmodern elements embedded in it. Stylistically speaking it is avant-garde and postmodern novel. In the present novel, the technique and style is extraordinary. In reality the central theme is World Peace. But there are other motifs too such as significance of marriage, sex and set of moral values in life, the negative effects of high-technology on human life, society and human relations particularly between individual and individual, individual and family and also individual and community. There is a great need of person to person contact in a family, society etc. though high technology has given many means of contacts such as mobile, phone, fax etc.., the significance of person to person contact cannot be undervalued and replaced by any other means. The need of a loving life-long companion with virtues of tolerance, adjustment, understanding and even sacrifices in both life partners are essential to pass the life happily. One may not agree with Vikram Seth's philosophy of 'mistrust of passion in life' and his view that in respect of love, one must give preference to reason over passion. It can't be denied that most significant decisions in one's life is taken by heart and not by mind.

Another device Seth uses for the purpose of distancing is humour. There are a number of tongue-in-cheek comments in his description of the relationships that the characters share with their respective pets. Schwartzenegger, Ed's pet iguana; Cult and Link (Janet's cals und Charlemagne (Liz's disgruntled puss) are used as characters in a comic, if somewhat absurd, context in life. Charlemagne, L1z's Siamese intensely jealous (and aging) cat, is as insecure as John is taken in as an orphan kitten, he feels threatened by John's intrusion into his territory. Charlemagne 'torments' John by making scratches on his trousers, ripping an official report to shreds and even urinating near his head. Llz is compelled to make a choice between her lover and her cat. Seth s literary genius is full of surprises. The irony with an undercurrent of humour is enhanced by the use of alliterative words 'solvent, sexy, then thrilling, thrifty and later in 'bosomy brunette'. The words are impinging for the artistic as well as literary implications. The desperation of this unheroic hero is indicated who being psychologically crippled is in search of a woman who is able bodied, wise as well as shy. There is a pun in the word bosomy'. It implies that she should be thrilling in bed and in life. Seth, the modern day writer, envisages other subversive as well as tolerant outlooks. His intentions are noble and fair and like Swift, Dryden and Austen, he uses wit sarcasm and irony to make readers aware of their follies. Nevertheless, the undercurrent of humour and a gentler treatment places him closer to Jane Austen. Seth is concerned about fostering better and healthier inter-personal relationships, where the beginning takes place is a family spreading further to a few friends and relatives. Marriage friendship then become the basic fulcrum of the microcosm only those turn victorious who through love and wisdom make themselves as well as other happy. Certain social evils are always rampant in the contemporary society, but through a better social system based on human values, one can hope for peace and satisfaction.

The protagonist of *The Golden Gate* as on account of his suspicious nature his lady love Liz who later married Phil. Nobody is responsible for the failure of John's love. John is himself responsible for his loneliness. The subject matter of this novel is not for one particular place but for all places and all times – love, life, work, profession, friendship, alienation, death, birth and pain. *The Golden Gate has* been hailed as the great Californian novel, because the themes it treats of: disillusionment from love, estrangement, discontentment of work place,

Silicon valley, nuclear bombs, one night stands homosexuality all these come together to form a very detailed picture of life in the coastal, cosmopolitan city of San Francisco, which represents the entire state of California in miniature.

In **The Golden Gate**, the social ill is existential; anguish and the aberrations found are in the form of lustful love, homosexuality, and lack of love, compassion and understanding. The situation is disturbing. Once a pessimistic approach is seeped into man's action, it 1s obvious that sooner or later he will experience void in his life. Lack of family and friends has bred an inferiority complex and low self-confidence in John; therefore, he needs the support of his friends even in personal matters like the choice of a life-partner. Janet is mocked at for not revealing her true emotions to John while she is helping him in finding a partner and madly pursues him, unmindful to the consequences of her efforts. She is frantically trying her best to conceal her pain and sufferings beneath the carapace of a sculptor and a musician.

Seth's characters are living in a world where sentimentality is taken to be moronic trait. As regards the tone of the novel, it is light-hearted and parodic. It "creates a complex web of sense and sensibility on various levels that ultimately results in extremely sophisticated parody". (20) Parody is present in the choice and elaboration of form and theme, in style, and technique. It thus operates at the structural level in the novel. The parody goes on to create inter textuality, not only of cross referential cultural connotations but also subtle inter textuality or literary style and forms. His style of sparse verse serves him well here. The characters are presented only in vignettes and they push the story forward, Seth adds the touch of sardonic humour by inserting the authorial voice in parenthesis. The style is ideal, both for the medium, which demands brevity, and for the theme, which demands levity and wit to keep it from sinking into a maudlin formlessness. Seth's wit is razor- sharp, and commendably, it never crosses the boundaries of good taste. The humour is also achieved by the use of anticlimax, antithesis, other figures of speech, Sometimes Seth created humour by emphasizing some small insignificant detail. Al of Seth's three novels carry a similar message, the consolidation of family, community and the nation, only the storyline and the locations differ.

Seth's sonnets retain the octave-sestet division, and due to the conversational tone, appear to be prose sentences, but the use of more feminine rhymes enables the lines to flow into each other seamlessly. The caesura is marked by an elliptical phrase, or a change in the thought. Seth gets so used to writing in this form that even the acknowledgement, the dedication and the table of contents have been versified. The novel successfully links a formal type of poetry with modern moral and spiritual dilemmas. The sonnet form is thus harnessed by Seth in a manner that it oscillates from being merely functional in taking the story forward to being rich in poetic eloquence. Seth's ability to forge an updated and precise medium is the nature of a vital artistic evolution, leading to a more heightened expression of experience than prose.

As a novel of plot or character, *The Golden Gate* is very thin indeed, in essence being little more than a succession of musical beds. To have attempted this tale in prose would have produced nothing more than a soap-operatic effect that would hardly have been worthwhile. But the medium Seth has chosen, sequential sonnets, by ils very nature calls for a certain dignity of approach as well as it demands from Seth an economy of delineation that ruthlessly leaves out the redundant, allows for a witty couplet at the end of each sonnet to break the monotony, and most importantly, calls attention away from the plot towards the form. Hollinghurst says, "It is truly hard to imagine a better vehicle for social verse narrative, which aims to be both reflective and lightly comic." (21) However the form is not in the nature of a deliberate volte-face from tradition. The choice is a natural one, considering the fascination that poetry exerts over Seth. Being a poet himself, it was natural for him to tum to a poet for inspiration. The pioneer of the novel in verse was Byron, whose Don *Juan* is a picaresque novel in verse. Pushkin acknowledges Byron as the model for his *Eugene Onegin*, and likewise, Seth acknowledges Pushkin, in a tribute incorporated into **The Golden Gate**, Byron's Don Juan is a satire on contemporary European life and civilization. Following Byron, Pushkin created in his novel a realistic portrayal of contemporary Russia. Following their lead, Seth chose to write, both satirically and realistically, a novel about contemporary California. In preparation for writing the novel, Seth read two translations of *Pushkin's Onegin*, attending especially to the Charles Johnston version, in which the translator followed the Pushkin's stanza throughout and approximated to Pushkin s inventiveness in rhyme and rhythm. The parallel in The Golden Gate runs as follows: Eugene is reincarnated as John.

The novel becomes a bildungsroman as it traces the growth of John from his childish, petulant phase to a maturity and an acceptance of life. The novel both begins and ends with John alone, but in the course of the tale John comes way towards understanding and tolerance, recognizing the value of such mundane institutions as friendship and marriage. The bildungsroman thus maps the journey of John from stumbling blindness to self discovery. Seth makes all the characters, and most of all John recognize that money, power, or any such wordily standards must not become ends in themselves.

The novel is like a tale in the oral tradition wherein the listeners are acutely involved in the story and at the same time aware that it is not for real. Seth sets out to tell a story, a story that is intimate, emotional and passionate. Yet, with the help of various distancing devices, the reader is kept aware of its fictional quality.

This technique has a dual advantage. It retains the reader's interest and sympathy: yet maintains sufficient objective correlative for analysis and a non-sentimental understanding of the author's material. In addition, the objective detachment on the reader's part is itself used to bring the reader closer to the novel: detachment is seen as undesirable. An accusing finger is pointed at all those who fear commitment. The reader himself is made to feel guilty for having an ironic vision that kept him at a distance from human contact.

Discussing George Eliot's dramatic use of the author's voice, Barbara Hardy says: "The narrative medium is composed of many voices. There is the direct speech of the author's pity, both for her own creatures and extending in generalization to lament and admiration for all humanity. There is the more detached voice of irony and analysis. There is the omniscient warn veiled and unveiled, working in the interests of aesthetic unity and dramatic irony." (22)

This is equally true of Seth's technique in *The Golden Gate*. Successfully combining the paradoxical qualities of sympathy and ironic perception, the novel carries an implicit warning: it warns the reader against having the sort of attitude that, for instance Eliot's Hollowmen represent. Having courage of one's conviction is the only hope, both in private as well as public life.

The Golden Gate as a verse novel falls into the category of "a narrative poem in several books, chapters or cantos which deals with the substance of modern life in much the same way as a work of prose fiction. They are set in a contemporary world with characters that are naturalistic rather than mythical or heroic. Generally Verse Novelists recognize the necessity of retaining the emotional power through music; imagery and concentration if the work in question is remain a poem." (23)

True to the tradition of a Verse Novel, it fulfills the criteria of a novel in thirteen chapters that deals with the contemporary world of California, which comprises neither mythical nor heroic but ordinary human beings, fraught with human frailties.

The Golden Gate is placed in the eighties of the last century. The poet describes the landscape around San Franscisco, the flowers, the shrubs and the trees. The episodes about olive picking and animal rearing could not have been located in different region. Even the habits of whales, gulls, pigeons and sea-lions are observed with the eye of a naturalist.

R.K. Kaul in his essay "Life and Love in California" states "that the structure of the novel is episodic and it resembles a chain in which each part is linked to what goes before and what comes after, but it has no centre. What gives continuously to the story is the Dorati connection". (24) Every character is in some way related to the Doratis. Their family or clan as the author calls them is an interesting sample for a historian of culture. They spend their leisure hours in Concert halls, movie theaters, play chess, scrabble and hunting kitsch; they have a passion for pets and they watch the TV for football matches. The younger members are sexually maladjusted. Mrs. Dorati senior has a compulsive wish to be a grandmother. In spite of individual variations, they are 70 a closely knit clan. They regularly go to Church to nod or pray. He says that Dorati's are fairly representative of the affluent middle class in contemporary America.

With regard to families, they do not loom large in the work. It appears that young unmarried ladies play the decisive roles. Nevertheless, old women play a major role on some occasions. Mrs. Dorati, wife of Mike Dorati and mother of Elizabeth, Ed and Sue is a loving, caring and anxious mother. This rheumatic lady fears that her children will prove to be fruitless crew. And she also foresees the danger of having a grand childless death. Fortunately, she lives to witness the marriage of Liz and Phil and the birth of a child. There is a glimpse of disintegrating family system in America. Readers are unable to come across the idea, gentle and good women- loved, loving unselfish, self-sacrificing wife and mother and the eternal virgin. Seth has given a portrayal of

American women who seem to be deficient in love, tenderness and even in any feminine fullness. Women in **The Golden Gate** do not seem to act as full individuals. Moreover, the increasing emancipation of women has nothing to ease the situation but rather tends to exacerbate it.

In *The Golden Gate,* the female characters especially are totally unlike the half-hearted caricatures one usually finds in poetry. They are full blooded, able-bodied, talented, creative, professionally successful, and psychologically stronger and more mature than the complexed and guilt-ridden male characters like Ed, Philip and John himself.

The Golden Gate, in short, is Seth's San Francisco novel – with the portrayal of alternative lifestyles, gender breakdowns and anti – military protests. It uses a fresh, unusual and extremely interesting experiment to look back to the ancient epic tradition, and bring it right up to date in modern California. It is a vibrant absorbing novel, notable for its vivid characterization as well as for its linguistic dexterity. It uses a fresh, unusual and extremely interesting experiment to look back to the ancient epic tradition, and bring it right up to date in modern California.

Refrences :-

1. Z.N.Patil's, The image of America in Vikram Seth's The Golden Gate, p-21.

2. C.N. Srinath's, Essays in Criticism, p-25.

3. Seemita Mohanty's, *A Critical Analysis of Vikram Seth's Poetry and Fiction, p-125.*

4. Seemita Mohanty's *A Critical Analysis of Vikram Seth's Poetry and Fiction, p135.*

5. Diana Trilling, *"The Image Women in Contemporary Literature,"* The Women in America, ed. R.J. Litton, Boston, Houghton Mifflin, 1965, p-61.

6. Supriya Karunakaran, *"Games in Novelist Play':* The Rebell of Vikram Seth in The Golden Gate and Shashi Tharoor in The Great Indian Novel," Fiction of Nineties, p-96.

7. Seth Vikram, *The Golden Gate*, New Delhi: penguin, 1986, p-52.

8. *The Golden Gate, p-29.*

9. Seth Vikram*: sonnet 1.1, The Golden Gate, Penguin Books 1986, p-3.*

10. Seth Vikram*: sonnet 5.3, The Golden Gate, Penguin Books 1986.*

11. Seth Vikram: *sonnet 2.55, The Golden Gate, Penguin Books 1986.*

12. Seth Vikram: *sonnet 7.21, The Golden Gate, Penguin Books 1986.*

13. Linda Hutcheon, *A Poetics of Postmodernist: History, theory, Fiction London*: Routledge, 1998, and p-8.

14. Pramod K.Nayar's *Vikram Seth, the Literary Genius: An Introduction, p- 17.*

15. *Pramod K. Nayar's and R.K. Dhavan's Vikram Seth, the Literary Genius: An Introduction, p-70.*

16. Oxford, Ed. *The New Oxford Dictionary of English,* Oxford: Oxford University Press, 2000.

17. *M. H. Abrahams, A Glossary, p128-129.*

18. Dante Gabriel Rossetti's *sonnets are examples of verbal image wedded to visual image, eliciting a mystical and artistic quality.* Rossetti's work included sonnets based on actual paintings, designed to reference them and enhance their appreciation, both visually and in literature.

19. *By lyrical, I am referring to "that kind of verse most readily associated with the chanted or sung origins of poetry." Wainwright, Jeffrey. Poetry: The Basics. Abingdon: Routledg, 2004.*

20. Karunakaran s., loc cit.

21. Hollinghurst Alan, *"In The Onegin Line,"* The *Times Literary Suppliment, July 4, 1986.*

22. S. Ramaswamy's *Vikram Seth's The Golden Gate: A Critical Study, p-69.*

23. Cuddon J.A , *The Penguin Dictionary of Literary Terms and Literary Theory, fourth edition, Penguin Books, p-965.*

24. R.K. Kaul's *Life and Love in California states, p-17.*

A Suitable Boy – A Study of Themes and Technique

3.(A) A Suitable Boy

In this chapter, Vikram Seth's craftsmanship as a novelist is explored, in the backdrop of the themes and styles of his novels. In the composition of the first novel *The Golden Gate*, he has chosen to employ verse as a means to give shape in words to his sense of inventiveness. But his other two novels have been composed only in prose, though in *A Suitable Boy* Seth's passion and interest in poetry is recurrently displayed in the form of couplets of Kakoli. In all the three novels, the theme of broken love recurs.

3.(B) Structure of A Suitable Boy

The novel has 19 sections, divided into a total of 477 small chapters, which are, on average, less than three pages long. As has been previously mentioned, this structure means that one scene reflects on another, rather than any depth being developed within an individual chapter. Interestingly, the longest parts of the novel, seven and thirteen (127 and 111pages respectively) arc the ones which depicts family life. In this way, the importance of the theme of the family to the novel is reflected in its form. *A Suitable Boy*, the novel of records, was no small achievement in 1993 at the time it was published, its vast amount of work did not fail to impress critics and reviewers all over the world: "more than 8 lakhs words knead in 478 sections of 19 parts in its 1347 pages weighing about fifteen hundred grams," (1) counted a very daring commentator. Planned therefore also with the intent to amaze the reader, it 1s not a work which lacks consistency. Written in a highly readable prose-style, well-sketched characters, a very neat and natty (central) plot it may look deceptively simple in its structure and contents. On the contrary, Vikram Seth wrote a monumental work which, although clearly set in a definite socio-historical context, makes direct reference to various elements and creates a new hybrid world. Seth does an admirable job handling the enormous cast of characters. Even the most minor characters are easily distinguishable from each other, and by the end of the book it is hard to avoid the feeling that you know these characters intimately, Seth deals deftly with the dizzying complexity of India's historical background. The bulk of the novel is used to portray a realistic picture of India. Vivid descriptions of the Pul Mela , the ordinary life of Rasheed's village, the horror of communal riots, a cricket match, the whole election procedure of campaigning polling and counting, all these lend the novel a very wide sociopolitical frame work. Apart from what Seth set out to do, what has been really done in *A Suitable Boy* is an outstanding achievement.

With the publication of his first prose fiction *A Suitable Boy (1993)*, "a sage of modern India", Seth proved himself a prose novelist of great strength and vision, a novelist of quality and commitment endowed with a capacity to sweep the great tradition of the novel in English into his broad perspective. Every work of literature creates its own world. Like Henry Fielding who stressed the idea of the novel is a comic epic in prose and sought to encompass the whole of the eighteenth century social life in his works. Vikram Seth attempts much the same canvas in his controversial novel *A Suitable*

Boy. In a volume exceeding thirteen hundred pages, Seth sets out to bring the entire post-independence India into his fictional vision. As a writer, Seth is conversant with life on various social levels. Well acquainted with both the high and the inferior sector of mankind, he portrays the mid twentieth century society in all its diversity which provided him with a fictional technique of contrasting characters and their life-styles with remarkable aesthetic effect.

3.(C) Plot of A Suitable Boy

A Suitable Boy focuses on the experiences and entanglements of four moderately rich Indian families connected through marriage or friendship at a period of time when India was experiencing her post independence turbulences. It is primarily about the social, religious and familial customs of India and her people with the numerous characters serving as tools to illustrate the veracity of these customs. It is structured into nineteen well-crafted sub sections that allow Seth to move back and forth while telling the story of four families- the Mehras, the Kapoors, the Khans, and the Chatterjees who are related to each other by marriage and friendship. Each family has a minimum of four members who in one way or the other experience a series of turbulent emotions, which slowly season them towards life and its adversities. In addition, to these individuals, there are also hordes of other characters who contribute either in a major or in a minor way, to the development and the progress of the plot line.

A Suitable Boy is wholly set in India of early 1950s when the process of nation building was taking place under the statesmanship of Jawaharlal Nehru. With regard to the main plot line, it centers on the question of finding a suitable partner for Lata, younger daughter of Mrs. Rupa Mehra. Three candidates present themselves; Amit Chaterjee, Bengal: poet and novelist, sophisticated, rich and a Brahmin. Kabir, a cricketer, dashing and handsome, but a Muslim, and Haresh, an energetic and bright young man determined to make a career for himself in the shoe manufacturing industry. Lata finally settles for Haresh.

But the main strength of the novel lies not in the business of matchmaking but in the depiction of social, physical, cultural, historical and romantic faces of India just after independence. Seth manages to interweave in a credible way all the larger themes of politics, culture, romance, society and history with the day to day ordinary human emotions of his true to life characters that have strong resemblance to Dickensian characters, over whom countless readers have laughed and cried. A multitude of characters and events through novel, the setting moves back and forth between the cities of Brahampur, which is fictional, and Culcutta and excursions to New Delhi, Kanpur and Luckhnow and to the remote village in the north Indian identity is strengthened and stretched to make it a representative of India as a whole. The wide sweep of the novel gives Seth a chance to portray life in factitious northern state of Purvapradesh in its various aspects. The investigator brings out the historical, political and romantic aspects of India of early 1950's that is portrayed in *A Suitable Boy.*

A Suitable Boy is about much more than a girl choosing a suitable husband. It is an exploration of all the trial that must be endured before enough strength has been acquired to do the right thing. It is an effective thought about life - the life not in slices but the life in its totality, in the Nehruvian era of Indian Civilization. **A Suitable Boy** is a landmark in Vikram Seth's career because it grounds him for the first time in Indian Soil. It is with **A Suitable Boy** that Seth focuses on India, an India that furnishes him with a muse, and a rather weighty one at that. Seth calls Mrs. Rupa Mehra (a character in the novel), "the muse of the project. She arrived one day and said, 'This is the story of me and my daughters'." (2) The novel, **A Suitable Boy** is not mere a story of few lines but there lies a moral behind them. A thematic study of Seth's novel seems to postulate that love posited in friendship is the most durable substation of human life, as compared to the "high joy or pain" that true love brings. This sentiment is more deeply explored in **A Suitable Boy**, in Lata's choice of a husband.

Seth explains how this came about, saying that he wanted to write about India and planned to write a series of five short novels. Instead, he wrote one rather long novel about India of the

1950s. Seth had planned that he would deal swiftly with this period and then go forward to the Sino-Indian war, the emergency etc., but he got stuck in that period .The more he researched it, the more the topics obsessed him-Zamindari Abolition, courtesans losing their sources of income, the British having left, the new kind of politicians moving in. It is also the quest of Vikram Seth, who was born in the year 1951, to find a niche in the history of Indo- England writing in India. *A Suitable Boy* has the body of Indian theme and clothes of Western novel. All important characters assemble at the wedding of Lata. The writing of *A Suitable Boy* is as much a labour of love for its author as it is a joy of readership for its readers.

3.(D) Themes of A Suitable Boy

Love is omnipresent; it is blind, uncares about customs and religion, profit or loss, and just happens at any time. This is what happens with the characters of *A Suitable Boy*. Lata falls in love with Kabir a Muslim boy; Maan falls in love with Saeeda Bai, a courtesan; Amit falls in love with Lata, short glimpses of love between Haresh Khanna and

Simran, Kakoli and Hans are also seen in the novel. At the very outset, we are revealed with the love of Lata and Kabir, in fact, we can say the first love of the novel. Lata, a student of English Literature at the University of Brahmpur, falls in love with Kabir Durrani, a fellow student, a cricketer and a Muslim. First they met at the Imperial Book Depot; beneath the Gulmohar tree then, in a music recital in Bhartendu Auditorium. Moreover, when Lata saw him in the cricket field, she was overwhelmed by his physical charms. It was here that Kabir's love nourished in Lata's heart and she regarded herself as one of the gopi, who instead of feeling jealous of Krishna's flute, had started envying Kabir's bat. Thus in few chance encounters, Lata falls in love with Kabir, thinking him to be a suitable husband but Kabir's insistence on marrying her after two years clinches the issue. The novel could have been on different path, if Kabir would have changed his mind of marrying after two years, otherwise it could have been ended in the elopement of Lata with Kabir. Since the difference of their religion will never make them marry with each other, at that time this would be the only one option left for them to work over.

Seth cares very much about his characters, the choice one makes is difficult but they have to obey. This is the way that Seth creates a worried of love not clouded with unrealistic dreams, and firmly entrenched in the reality of life.

Maan is the next prey who is caught in the web of Love. This time the love is with a famous courtesan Saeeda Bai, lived not far from Prem Nivas, who came from a family of singers and courtesans and had a tine, rich and powerful emotional voice. She was a woman of thirty five but her fame as singer had been spread outwards from Brahmpur. Maan who had spent two Holi's in Benares, knew her fame, but had not heard her sing. But his third Holi was this time at Prem Nivas where he saw Saeeda Bai and was totally overwhelmed by her ghazals. Maan, the son of Minister of Revenue, was so affected by Saeeda Bai's recitation of final couplet, that he raised his arms helplessly towards her and was surprised at his doing. He became so blind in his love that he forgot about the reputation of his father in the society, didn't care about his mother's illness and stay tuned to that courtesan, not only this he even started taking tuitions from Abdur Rasheed for Urdu so that he can write to Saeeda Bai who can only read Urdu, though he had to manage the rural life at Rasheed's village in Debaria he didn't care about that. Here a question arises in one s mind -From where does he get the strength to learn a language and revolt against his father's decision of marrying a girl they have chosen for him? The answer that comes at once to the mind is his love for Saeeda Bai. This love made him a rebel, a murderer and a big loser in life. A young boy sometimes chooses a wrong path, probably at this age of Maan. They create a world of their own and all the decisions they take pretends to be the final and appropriate one, no one can show them the mirror of truth, the one who tries, becomes the enemy who don't want to see them happy, no matters if they are their own well wishers or their parents. Later they come to their senses but when they lose a lot from life as Maan suffered. This time he chooses his family upon his love.

Seth has succeeded in presenting the cruel realities of life that one faces in one's life. In some cases love gives life tame and wisdom but the thing that matters is the right choice of love as if Saeeda Bai could have belonged to a decent cultural and of appropriate caste, the result of Maan's love might have been accepted and appreciated. Since, a courtesan is considered to be or a very low category in the society and have got no right to love or marry in her life, Saeeda Bai has to keep herself' away from it and she knows her limitations. She never tried to cross her limits. Maan's passion for Saeeda Bai is also seen from different angles. It is mostly depicted as amusing, endearing, and titillating. However, during the scene in which Saeeda Bai and Tahmina Bai cheer themselves up with imitations of their clients, Saeeda Bai does "quite a good impression of Maan making desperate love" (3) and this reminds us with a jolt of the commercial nature of their relationship and seems to demean not just Maan but Saeeda Bai as well.

Love is a gift of God; no one can escape from the grace of it. Amit Chaterjee, the witty cosmopolitan English poet, who did well, is the authorial persona; especially when it comes to his ideas about the aesthetics of the novel and writing in

English. He has a secret desire for Lata; he started enjoying her company as when Amit gave a small garland of white bela flowers to Lala she puts it unselfconsciously in her hair. This pleased Amit very much and he accepted that she may be more intelligent than her sisters, but he was she's not sophisticated. She's the nicest girl he had met for a long time. He gave her compliments that she has a nice smile, he gives her a New Year kiss and finally he proposes Lata: you are quite right. In that base will you marry me? Lata dropped her cup. It fell on the floor and broke." (4) In this case love is one sided Lata did know that Amit was fond of her, but her chief emotion at the kiss was still astonishment. Moreover she tells Malati that she cannot imagine herself as his wife at all; further she recommends that they are too alike and if his mind is on a book, he will have no time for her as sensitive people are usually insensitive.

Apart from these love couples, Seth has presented before us very short glimpses of love of Kakoli and Hans Rasheed, Ishaq and Firoz's secret love for Tasneem; Haresh and Simran's love.

Though these are presented on a very small scale but they exist in the novel maintaining their vitality. These characters have succeeded in making their own place in the mind of readers. These all together make the novel weighty and entertaining. Kakoli had not at first been ecstatic about Schubert, her tastes running more to Chopin, whom she played with heavy rubato and gloom. But now that she was accompanying Hans singing she had grown to like Schubert more and more. The same was true about her feeling for Hans, whose excessive courtliness bad at first amused her, then irked her, and now reassured her. Hans, for his part, was as smitten but Kuku as any of her mushrooms had ever been. But he felt that she took him lightly, only returning one in three of his calls. Here, the lovers pretend the same taste, see the life with the same angle. Though Kakoli is crazy and of dominative nature but, then Hans manages it, this way the love finds its path. Tasneem, is the one in the novel who has got three admirers: the first one Ishaq, who liked Tasneem and for her happiness presented her a parakeet. When she calls him 'Ishaq Bhai', he resists her to do so, may be because of is secret love for her which he could not disclose because of

Saeeda Bai's terror. But one thing is clear that he is definitely a secret lover of Tasneem. His thoughts about Tasneem's beauty can be read in these lines "Ishaq looked at her and thought that 'gazelle-like' really did suit Tasneem. Delicate -featured, tall and slender, she did not resemble her elder sister. Her eyes were liquid and her expression tender. She was lively, but always seemed to be on the point of taking flight." (5)

Firoz is the next one, who is a secret admirer of Tasneem. He talks coolly with Biboo because it would have been impossible otherwise for him, to communicate with Tasneem. Though he had seen her only twice, yet she fascinated him; and he felt that she must surely feel something for him, for although her letters were gentle and discreet, the very fact she wrote them without her sister's knowledge, required courage. On lie eve of Moharram when Firoz saw Tasneem sitting at the back of the room, she looked very beautiful in her a fawn-colored salwsar-kameez as delicate as the first time he had seen her. Her eyes filled with tears.

Rasheed, Tasneem's tuition teacher also comes in the line of her admirers. In a conversation of Maan and Saeeda Bai it is disclosed that Rasheed had been sending strange letters to Tasneem which are offensive. On the other side, we hear from Rasheed that "I know that you and Saeeda Bai and others, including important people on the government, are trying to get me married to her." (6) Further, he tells that he will marry only if his marriage with Tasneem will be kept secret from the rest of the family. Without knowing the reality, Rasheed is making castles in air; neither Tasneem is interested in him or Saeeda Bai. Tasneem respects Rasheed as his teacher and that is all. Rasheed's thinking that Tasneem loves him and that Saeeda Bai wants him to marry her is totally a waste of time. This is what one sees in this world. People very often fall in love, without knowing the truth of their love and when they fail they either and harm others or themselves. Haresh and Simran's love is revealed in the novel, a love that deals religion as Simran is a Sikh and Haresh is a Lala, which among the Sikhs was something of a term of contempt for Hindus. Both loved each other but their family was not in favour of it.Though Simran's sister liked Haresh but that was not enough. She knew that Haresh loved her sister faithfully but no one can fight against the fate.

Seth tells about Zamindari Bill and it's far reaching impact on the nation and the hurdles and the challenges the policy makers had to encounter in enacting and implementing the law has been so accurately recorded in the novel. The main story takes place in an imaginary and fictional north Indian state called Purvapradesh the Chief Minister of which is Sharma and the revenue and home ministers of the state are Mahesh Kapoor and Agarwal respectively. Vikram Seth has structured this fictional state Purvapradesh in such a way that it stands for the whole of north India in all aspects such as, culture, religion, society, geography and politics. Zamindari abolition bill is the brain child of Mahesh Kapoor, the revenue minister of the state who is a staunch loyalist of Nehru and strong supporter of his secular principles. In the loosely narrated story of romance between a Muslim boy, by name, Kabir and a young lady Lata, a Brahampur university student numerous episodes dealing with various other themes have been incorporated without affecting the course, effect and flow of the main story. One such sub theme of historical importance is Zamindari Abolition Bill. In the history of modern independent India, Zamindari Abolition Act turns out to be a milestone legislation which played a pivotal role in streamlining land related matters. It is preceded by the annexure of small kingdoms to Indian union, by the then Home Minister of India Vallapai Patel, known as iron man of India. Even after that, Zamindars were in possession of vast acreage of lands and sprawling estates where landless labourers toil hard to earn their livelihood. There is every possibility for the emergence of a situation where people belonging to the lower strata of society have to continue to remain as landless laborers and earn their bread.

In British India, such a scenario, where the economically, socially and culturally underprivileged sections were denied justice was prevalent. But even after attaining freedom, when some sections of the nation live in absolute luxury and the rest of the nation languish in poverty and starvation, it cannot be defended and justified. With a view to equalizing the imbalances, disparities and discriminations among different sects of people in every sphere economy and agriculture, Zamindari Abolition Bill was introduced. Mahesh Kapoor a strong follower of Nehru and his principles of secularism, and socialism is strongly under the impression that it will bring about equality in the state and the gap between the haves and the have-nots would be bridged to a good extent. Even if it means that very influential landlords and powerful zamindars are to lose major portions of their estates, fields and land, Mahesh Kapoor does not step behind. One of the affected Zamindars Nawab Sahib of Baitar is a long time and close friend of the revenue minister Mahesh Kapoor.

Notwithstanding that, there is no friction between Nawab Sahib of Baitar and Mahesh Kapoor. The bill, which later becomes a law, imposing a ceiling on the possessions of lands by zamindars and landlords do not damage the mature and refined friendship between the duo. Mahesh Kapoor in the process has to incur the displeasure and wrath of the likes of Raja of Marh who strongly believes that the minister is responsible for the deprivation of their lands. But Mahesh Kapoor is committed to the goals of anti-feudalism, secularism and elimination of zamindari system. On personal front, he is also a determined fighter against feudalism, the evils of communalism and the growing menace of corruption. He is a man of commitment, honesty and integrity. At one point, when Raja of Marh attempts to bribe him to prevent the passage of zamindari abolition bill, he ruthlessly tackles him, by coming hard on him. And he is a man who is capable of outweighing personal relationships for the betterment of larger, general objectives and close friendship with the Nawab Sahib of Baita also helps him in this commitment, in the sense that Mahesh Kapoor's moral principles do not come in the way of their friendship.

In *A Suitable Boy* Zamindari Abolition Law, a historically important legislation finds its expression in the work. Under the Zamindari Abolition Bill, five years of continuous tenancy is enough to establish the tiller's right to the land. The agricultural fields of land lords and Zamindars have been ploughed by labourers who are landless and a portion of the yielding they would be given for their labour and the rest would be submitted to the landlords and Zamindars. This had been the custom and tradition during British regime. With the implementation of Zamindar Abolition act, agricultural workers without their own land toiling hard and long on others' fields for their survival would be entitled to claim their right over the fields and the owners of fields who happen to be Nawabs, Rajas and Landlords would be severely hit by the legislation. They are up in arms against this legislation and they bend over backwards to prevent it from coming into force. Once it is passed in legislature and the governor gives his assent to it, Nawabs, Rajas and the Landlords losing their properties and struggling hard like other common men for their existence and livelihood will be inevitable. Realizing the danger they will be in, they challenge the constitutional validity of the legislation in Brahampur high court. Heated arguments are witnessed in the court both for and against the legislation. G.N. Bannerjee, the counsel for the landlords, presented his argument in the following way.

> "My Lords, the entire way of
> life of this state is sought to
> be altered by the executive of
> this state through legislation
> that runs in express and
> implied contradictions to the
> constitution of the country.
> The act that seeks, in no
> citizenry of purva Pradesh is
> the Purva Pradesh Zamindari
> abolition and Land Reform
> Act in 1951 and it is my
> contention and that of other
> counsel for the applicants that
> this legislation, apart from
> being patently to the
> detriment of the people, is
> unconstitutional and therefore
> null and void." (7)

Casteism is also a big fact for the politician of India,
as well as religion and secularism. In Indian society
caste is an important thing for marriages and social

life. In **A Suitable Boy** the politics of caste and racial discrimination of society has been successfully charted by Seth. Vikram Seth realistic, orderly narrative recounts the major up heaves in the Indian subcontinent such as the partition of India the subsequent animosity between the Hindu and Muslim, the caste system untouchability and abolition of Zamindari system and its consequences. Seth describes the class division on the basis of caste and economical condition of free India. Seth describes the rise of middle class he still includes many characters from all. Seth highlights the includes the fictional zamindari abolition Bill in his **A Suitable Boy.** Mahesh Kapoor in his role as Revenue Minister is instrumental in bringing forth the Zamindari abolition Bill which would take the land from rich landlords with large and unproductive land holding in the state and would distribute it among the poor, landless farmers, Even though his friend the Nawab of Baitar would stand to lose from this legislature.

It is worthwhile to mention here that though Seth advocates for Indian sensibility nourishing its social and religious perspective through his characters, he could not dare to put on before readers inter-caste marriage between Kabir Durrain and Lata because of result and communal mania in 1951-1952. Therefore Lata lastly selected Haresh as her husband because he is not only from same caste but also hard working, intelligent and working class self made Indian man.

One major theme in **A Suitable Boy, is** religious intolerance. It started with romantic relationship between Lata and Kabir. Lata Mehra in a few chance encounters happens to meet Kabir, a fellow-student from a similar class at Brahmpur University. But since he has an ambiguous first name she doesn't know untill later that he is a Muslim. Kabir Durani is a student of history at the University and is the son of an eccentric, though brilliant, mathematics professor. Their passionate encounters are restricted to boat rides up the Ganges and brief stolen kisses. When his identity is revealed, she is at once aware that a relationship with him is "impossible, knowing the clear taboos against Hindu-Muslim miscegenation in the specific cultural and religious practices of the Indian subcontinent. Her friend Malati's initial response to Kabir's Muslimness exemplifies such awareness when she advises Lata to "better drop him" (8) as well as Lata's own reiteration at various points in the novel that this relationship is "pointless" and futile. Don't you know", she asks Kabir, What it (the notion of marriage to a Muslim) means in my family." (9) However. Kabir's reaction to the seemingly impossible social taboo against Hindu-Muslim marriage is a secular surprise that this should not be an issue at all. "You love me. And I love you that's all that matters," he avows in a classic affirmation of love transcending ail differences of culture, class, religion, race or caste.

However, Lata's mother Mrs. Rupa Mehra's hysterical outburst when she finds out that Lata has been not only "seen with a boy" but one who's a "Muslim" clearly bears out Lata's misgivings, that her upper-caste Hindu family will never accept her relationship with Kabir. "Is he a Parsi", Rupa Mehra asks Lata hopefully because even though the thought was odious it was not so "calamitously horrifying." (10) In the specific context of caste society, while the idea of marrying a non-khatri Hindu is transgressive in itself, the very notion of Hindu-Muslim marriage is unspeakable and unthinkable for Rupa Mehra. It is arguably the most pre-eminent taboo concerning marriage in the subcontinent as it rests on ideas of purity, pollution and religious exclusivism. Moreover, when Mrs. Mehra discovers that Kabir's mother is suffering from a mental illness, it only confirms her "othering" of Muslims. "Muslim and mad." she warns Lata as if the two words are synonyms for each other. Notably, Seth does not denounce Rupa Mehra as a monstrous abnormal, but a woman representative of her class, caste and generation.

Consequently, she takes Lata to Calcutta to remove her from the polluting and threatening presence of Kabir. Lata giving up her 'unsuitable' Muslim suitor is however not solely based on Mrs. Mehra's opposition on religious grounds. Lata shares none of her mother's Caste or religious prejudices. Initially Lata suggests to Kabir that they should run away together. However, Kabir does not elope with Lata and this is not really because he foresees the difficulties of an interreligious marriage in India of the 1950, but because he has plans of his own upward mobility. He intends joining the Indian Foreign Service and sees Lata's impulsive decision to elope as impractical.

Inter-community or inter-racial love has been much discussed in the European novel. Cross cultural desire has always been effectively used as a way of bridging cultural, religious or social boundaries within the nation as well as across national borders. Peter Hulme demonstrates how such love plots articulate the "idea of cultural harmony through romance. "Within the tradition of Indian writing in English" *Arundhati Roy's The God of Small Things* is perhaps the most famous example of this Literary convention romance here is figured between the upper- caste Syrian Christian woman und the "untouchable" Paravan, Velutha. The passionately celebrated sexual encounter between Aurora, the Catholic, and the Abraham, the Jew in *Salman Rushdie's The Moor's Last Sigh*, which results in the birth of the "Jewholic anonymous" protagonist Moor, is another well-known literary example of inter-community desire. While Aurora and Abraham's romance soon sours, their coming together at all is in keeping with Rushdie's larger celebrations of cultural hybridity and inter-mixing as a way or transgressing the boundaries of communities. Seth's representation of Lata-Kabir relationship and the unconventional trajectory it takes in the novel is against the backdrop of this literary and cinematic convention. His seemingly traditional closure appears as a refusal to repeat the notion that love or desire can bridge the gap between communities. He disallows the utopian function of inter-religious love as a mode of cultural syncretism and tolerance. In this refusal, he is not much different from many other secular critics. For example, Aijaz Ahmad notes that:

Novels of this kind (that figure love across social and political divisions) come to an end in one of two ways, the more pervasive in modern fiction is the characteristically 20th century, optimistic and ideologically permissive conclusion in which the lovers walk away into the sunset, or at least find in each other the solace that the external world of social relation denies them. Cinema from Hollywood to Bombay is full of such endings, in which love conquers all and easy personal solutions are offered for intractable social conflicts. But fictions of transgression, especially sexual transgression, also end in another way, very familiar since the 19th century novel, in which the wages of Sin are death and the individual is helpless against the overwhelming weight of social hypocrisy. (11)

Seth's novel seems to refuse both forms of closure. *A Suitable Boy* does not provide the "walking away into the sunset kind of ending" that Ahmad and others have derided, in presenting the confusion as Lata's well thought out choice of a calmer, less frantic love (and not just a yielding to the forces of patriarchal orthodoxy), this novel also does not offer a simplistic patriarchal narrative of the inevitable futility of such romances. Set as it is against the backdrop of emerging Hindu – Muslim conflict, Seth disallows romance the performative potential of being a way out of intractable religious conflict in India. Within the terms of this novel, romance is too easy and simplistic a solution to what is seen as difficult social conflicts.

A Suitable Boy attempts communal conflict in post partition Brahmpur, at an epic scale to represent India as the great crowd, several scenes of group violence or collective anarchy are depicted in the novel including a student protest turned violent, a Hindu mela gone wrong, and two scenes of communal violence. Seth's treatment of the two moments of religious violence, his representation of communal conflict in the early years after independence shows his concern Significantly, Seth chooses to set these riots against the backdrop of the Hindu revivalist movements in no small measure by State functionaries like L.N. Aggarwal, the Congress Home Minister of Purva Pradesh. In a thinly veiled fictional reconstruction of the Babri- Masjid conflict, Seth constructs a scenario of, dispute over a historic mosque that is believed to stand on the site of an ancient Shiva temple. The Raja of Marh becomes the representative of a nascent Hindu nationalist movement in the early fifties. The decadent Raja who is quite happy to consort with Muslim courtesans like Saeeda Bai had decided to build a Shiva temple "to stand cheeck by jaw with the grand mosque constructed by Emperor Aurangzeb two-and-a-half centuries ago on the ruins of an earlier temple to Shiva". (12)

The first riot takes place against this setting of an emergent Hindu nationalist movement in the early fifties. The Raja lays the foundation stone of the temple-as a consequence, the Imam of the Alamgiri Mosque gives an inflammatory speech to his congregation on Friday, and in a typical instance of cyclical violence, a riot breaks out between the Hindus and Muslims of the city over clashing religious symbols. The call for prayer from the mosque is interrupted by the sound of a conch. "Normally", Seth states, "such a thing might have been angrily shrugged off but not today". (13) Seth clearly demonstrated how fundamentalist discourses play a huge role in the transformation and crystallization of religious identities over and above all other identities in moments of conflict. However, significantly he also indicts the state for its complicity in allowing the violence to take place in the first instance when it could so easily have been controlled or averted. About the same time, Brahmpur also becomes the scene for a caste conflict between the traders of Misri Mandi and the shoemakers who are largely of the Jatav cast. L. N. Aggurwal. The Home Minister-by reason of his own caste affiliations-despite the sound advice of the District Magistrate, decided to deploy a vast majority of policemen for controlling the uprising of the low-caste Jatavs; as a result there are only a handful of policemen left near the site of the mosque and temple when the riot breaks out. The police are forced to fire at the Muslim mob due to the lack of an adequate deterrent police force and several people lose their lives. In Seth's representation of this first riot, then, the State is undoubtedly held culpable for its passivity and mismanagement of the situation. This justifies the narrator's pithy statement: "some riots are caused, some bring themselves into being". (14) Through this recreation of the scene of communal violence and in the effort to outline its causes, Seth clearly indicts Hindu nationalists as well as the state for rising religious intolerance in his present.

In Seth's fictional world, Aggarwal becomes the fictional representative of a Hindu chauvinist perspective. His hatred for his parliamentary rival Begum Abida Khan, one of the leaders of the landowners party is transformed into a hatred of all Muslims who, if "Nehru were not so soft-hearted", would have been dealt with "properly a few years ago". His revenge takes on the form of literally attempting to cleanse the nation by evicting the Muslim "other" the Nawab's family-from their ancestral home. His anti-Muslim remarks-"they were all fanatics, these Muslins, who appeared not to realize that they were here in this country on sufferance"-has become the commonsense expression of many middle-class Indians today; but in making him express these views, Seth is not being ignorant or anachronistic. Rather, he is concerned to demonstrate that Hindu nationalism is not a new and surprising strain of Indian political life that it has always been a latent element even within the self-professedly "secular" Congress, Speaking of Hindu hardliners" in the congress, especially the followers of Tandon.

Seth clearly holds the Congress responsible for "nepotism, corruption inefficiency, complacency even in those early days"(15). He cites a letter from Nehru- who makes two brief appearances in the novel even though his vision of secularism permeates the entire text-expressing a similar concern about the congress party:

> I feel that the Congress is rapidly drifting away from its moorings and more the wrong kind of people, or rather people who have the wrong kind of ideas, are gaining influence in it. The public appeal of the Congress is getting less and less; it may and probably will, win elections. But, in the process, it may also lose its soul............. (16)

Consequently, Seth's novel suggests that an appreciation of those initial years after independence is crucial for an understanding of the emergence and politics of the Hindu Right in contemporary India.

Marriage is the sole theme of the novel as the novel commences with a wedding and terminates with a marriage. The only difference is the earlier marriage of Mrs. Rupa Mehra's elder daughter Savita and the later one is of her younger daughter Lata. Marriages are of three types: Arranged marriage, Love marriage and Court marriage. In the novel neither love marriage is focused nor is any preference given to court marriage. All the emphasis has been put on arranged marriage. Majority of arranged marriages in the novel gives a view of the mentality of the people in the post -Independence India. In the novel Vikram Seth has shown different types of marriages. Majority of the people believe that love has no place before marriage. They don't believe in love which happens before marriage. According to them it's only an infatuation that a young boy and a young girl feel. Love is the destination that one can achieve only when one gets married. Moreover, the marriage must be within the caste and should be the arranged one. Marriage is a commitment for the entire life that the mates have to follow, so it should be decided with a cool mind and any kind of haste can prove the marriage distasteful. All the marriages shown in the novel gives the strength to test the accuracy of its subservient existence. The four families in the novel the Mehra's, the Khans, the Chatterji's and the Kapoors- all are result of arranged marriages. Vikram Seth along with the emphasis on the arranged marriage has shown the readers different images of marriage, and for this, he uses his characters as the medium to show the realities of life. The novel touches the life of ordinary people and also the VIPs.

Dr. Kishen Chand Seth is re-married to Parvati. He represents and symbolizes the advancement, possessiveness and forwardness of men in taking second wife ravishly, without caring their own age, family and children. They always prefer an unmarried woman, rather than stretching the helping hand towards a widowed or divorced or a woman having children. Dr. Kishen Chand Seth in the novel is one of them. His marriage with young

Parvati gave a great shock to Mrs.Rupa Mehra (daughter of Dr.Kishen Chand Seth): "The marriage with Parvati (which have shocked not just his family but Brahmpur at large because of disparity of age)." (17) It is the dominative nature that matters a lot rather than caring about the social rituals, customs and family; in other words selfishness of a person who becomes blind in his/her own happiness.

There exists another case of re-marriage, of Abdhur Rasheed, a tutor. He is married to his elder brother's widow with one daughter, accepted her as his wife and had a daughter of his own from her. This time here the marriage is being forced upon the individual by his own mother for the sake of her daughter-in-law and her granddaughter. Rasheed wanted to refuse her but he didn't have the heart to do so, a promise that was no doubt good in it but that had tied his life even before he had begun to taste freedom. Among the Muslims four marriages are considered to be legal. That may be the reason that Rasheed's father had a step wife, with her a son called Netaji. Begum Abida Khan, member of Democratic Party, proved to be more effective than her husband in social and political causes. With the coming of the partition, her husband decides to leave India and go to Pakistan, later he went to Iraq on a visit to the holy shrines of the Shias and decided to live there for a few more years. Three years passed but he didn't return. Abida Khan is here in India serving for the country and people, whereas her husband is far from her. This marriage follows separation but there still exists bond of love in both the hearts. No details are given in the novel about their contacts, only it is revealed that after his departure they had talks on phone only twice or thrice. Since they are apart from each other they are tied with thread of marriage and this cannot be forgotten. Vikram Seth conveys that separation cannot erase love from the hearts; it will linger till the life ends. Marriage is a commitment that cannot be broken so easily.

Next, is the marriage of a politician Mr. Mahesh Kapoor, Revenue Minister of the state of Purva Pradesh; he has a very busy schedule, busy life style and privilege to his work first, works intensely in the office and in house; Mrs. Kapoor is a good mother and a wonderful gardener but for her husband, she is not a suitable wife for him. As she is superstitious, cannot speak English she is nothing but a waste. When she was alive Mr. Kapoor never realized her good qualities, soon after her death he realized the importance of his wife that he never paid any attention. Mahesh Kapoor was amazed by how many people had come to attend the chautha of his wife, whom he always thought of as being a silly, superstitious and narrow- minded lady. He realized that she was the garden of Prem Nivas, Veena' s music Maan's generosity the survival of some refugees, Pran's asthma and Bhasker's great grandmother. Indeed for all the Minister of Revenue's impatience, she was his regret. This is a marriage in which husbands are considered as rod and the wife must obey her husband without caring about her own feelings and emotions, Mahesh Kapoor never cared about his wife's sentiments, on the other hand his wife served him her entire life as a slave; serving him and his children without any complain and revolt. Marriage means fulfillment of emotions and sentiments from both the sides but here it was one sided. Though Mahesh Kapoor never gave his wife any kind of physical harassment yet something was lacking in Mrs. Kapoor's life, which has to be filled by Mr. Kapoor, and that is his attention towards her. This marriage can be categorized in the category of a successful marriage, as both loved each other, though there was some vacuity. The reality that Vikram Seth has shown us that the wives of ministers usually undergo this type or frustration as Mrs. Kapoor went through. But here the politician is very loyal towards his work and his country.

Saviti and Pran Kapoor's marriage is presented as the most appropriate and the suitable one. Pran kapoor is a professor and a very intelligent human being. He has all the essential qualities that a man must possess. lie is an obedient son of his parents, loving and caring husband, and a devoted professor as for him Honesty is the best policy. Pran Kapoor is the only one character in the novel that is enriched with all the good qualities, his wife Savita also proves to be a decent wife, an obedient daughter, a simple ordinary woman who lives a simple life with her husband sharing his worries and happiness. In marriage with Savita, he has proved to be a wonderful husband. In the whole novel this is the one couple with a proper understanding among them and is never complaining to each other, a person gains his reputation from the society in which he lives. Society has its own rules and regulations which the person belonging to it has to obey. If he doesn't follow those rules he is considered a rebellion. The quality differs from person to person.

Society deals with all sorts of people good and bad. Seth has shown a small specimen of this kind of love which is a reality: young boys very often become the toys in the hands of time and become indecisive, become confused between true love and infatuation as Maan's love for Saeeda Bai is considered as Maan's infatuation. He was infatuated more by her sweet voice, and this sweet voice was gifted to Saeeda Bai along with her physical beauty. So, he was impressed by her physical charms and good voice as well. Whatever may be the situation, Seth gives a perfect turn to his characters and that is the reason how Maan finally decides to forget his love. *A Suitable Boy*, it seems, is more interested in the interaction between people in society than in the psychology of the individual. The value given to the self-expression in the west is something associated with Romanticism. Although it is nineteenth-century novels to which *A Suitable Boy* is usually compared because of its panoramic depiction of society, in one respect all Seth's writing is more akin to the classicist spirit of the eighteenth-century and its emphasis on universal experiences and values. It is ultimately universal death. Rasheed and Mrs. Kapoor both die during the course of the novel, Firoz, Pran, Bhasker, and Maan are also all in death's shadow at some point. Through these experiences Mahesh Kapoor comes to realize the value of his wife and his son, Maan to understand that passion bas to be controlled.

Malati and Maan are rebels. However their rebellions differ in that Maan rebels against his family and Malati against society. The more they resist, the more display of power they are exposed to. Yet, neither Malati nor Maan has any complaints. They do not care what people say or think, but they just do whatever they want. They are modern, courageous and bold young person's: Malati, has been brought up by a modern mother and because she is herself educated in the Western style, is a very broad-minded, rebellious, sell-confident and self-contained girl. Education, though it is also a tool of the colonialist for providing domination, in cases like Malati's, can be means of independence as well. Malati saw in books she read at school the examples of what she has been taught by her mother at home of individuality and Malati has taken her share of those ideas and attitudes. Therefore, she has educated herself as an independent woman whom no one can ever colonize.

Female subordination is another theme of *A Suitable Boy*. In *A Suitable Boy*, Lata falls in love with Kabir but she cannot decide herself and marry without her parents' permission and other male members of family. Lata's love points towards ever expanding cultural lag that Lata did not get ready for arrange marriage easily. Indian people prefer boys because of their value in all professional activities to be higher and after marriage a boy continue residing with his parents supporting them. In contrast, a girl drains family resources, especially when a large dowry goes with her to concerning husband this sort of mentality prevails in Indian society. Vikram Seth depicts male centric society of India in *A Suitable Boy*, for example Mahesh Kapoor and Nawab Shahib of Baitar praise the ideal household space like that were people live inside the particular jobs assigned to them. The state of Muslims ladies and lower rank ladies like Kachheru's better half and how man centric society constrained on their life are additionally depicted in this Novel.

In ancient time in our country women had full respect and honour. But after sometime they lost it. They lost their freedom, but inside of the boundary wall and became victim of inequality and atrocity. Seth thinks for betterment of the women of Indian society advocates for the rights of woman in the novel. Seth is against the inequality, atrocity, dishonour and exploitation of woman community in male dominated society. Ila is another women in this novel who disparages the domestic confinement, transgresses the feminine bounds and gets in male domain. She is related to Chatterjees and has pursued an academic career in spite of strong pressure from her family to give up it.

Saeeda, having suffered painful sexual exploitation wishes no such thing for Tasneem, her daughter from a disgraceful life. By her own protectionism she denied Tasneem any outside contest or association with normal people. This 'non awareness' is made in a beautiful feminine quality. "An assertion is in young brides to preserve the family system." (18) Lata and Kabir and Tasneem are conditioned to attain this muted consciousness. Saeeda Bai and Tasneem are not suitable for living a respectable life which other woman live. Vikram Seth, like other feminist, speaks in the favour of women's right, inequality, atrocity, empowerment and all kinds of social, cultural, political and economical freedom. He wants that the government should provide all kinds of facilities to all women for the betterment of the family, society and the country.

In *A Suitable Boy*, Vikram Seth has allowed his heroine the opportunity of choosing between three men who are totally different from each other in their appearance as well as in their behavior. And in keeping with this tradition, the courtship also takes place in three very different ways. Kabir Dumani the handsome and dashing Muslim student is the first to enter Lata's life. Their love affair starts in typical storybook fashion, continues along the same lines, but sadly does not end with them living happily ever after:

"She smiled to herself now, not aware of her surrounding. Still holding the book, she looked up. And this was how a young man, who had been standing not far from her, was included, unintentionally, in her smile. He was pleasantly startled, and smiled back at her. Lata frowned at him and looked down at the page again. But she could not

concentrate on it."
(19)

In spite of Kabir's princely looks, and his capacity to sweep the heroine off her feet, Kabir is no knight in shinning armour. On the contrary, according to Mrs. Rupa Mehra, he is the most unsuitable of them all and whom Lata should avoid like plague. But Lata is unable to resist his charm and his oozing sexuality and falls desperately and passionately in love with him:

".......She was drowsingly entranced by the sight of Kabir dressed completely in white, shirt unbuttoned at the collar, capless and with ruffled hair, running in to bowl or standing at the crease wielding his bat with what seemed like easy skill. Kabir was an inch or two under six feet, slim and athletic, with a fair to wheatish complexion, an aquiline nose, and black wavy hair. Lata did not know how long she sat there, but it must have been for more than half an hour." (20)

Seth introduces us to the world of courtesans also. He touches upon the social and sexual exploitation of women like Saeeda Begum. While generally absorbed in her professional duties, Saeeda Bai is a woman of the lower level-one without social dignity, without resources: she has therefore to resort to the temporary pleasures of drink and sex. Seth brings in the contrast of the sacred versus profane love anti-thesis. Saeeda Bai plays a rotten game while Lata goes in search of true, noble love. There is a void in Saeeda Bai's life so she is in search of meaning and hence symbolic of man's existential loneliness in the universe. In spite of her relations with Maan, she is essentially a lonely woman who finds escape from boredom in liquor and sex. It is only with Maan that life comes to have some meaning for her but even so she is far from satisfaction. Her building up of a paradise with Maan shows that she has found an ideal companion in him, hut their separation again leaves her as lonely as she ever was. Maan and Saeeda Bai are representatives of a sordid, unstable alliance steeped in social disgrace. Maan's sexual and emotional involvement with Saeeda comes to a melodramatic end. When he visits Saeeda after accompanying his father on his election campaign tour, he sees his best friend Firoz with her.

Through a scene reminiscent of popular Hindi Cinema, the intensely jealous Maan has doubt on his friend for her involvement with Saeeda. He stabs Firoz and then stumbles into the dark of the night, covered with blood. Maan is arrested and charged with dangerous assault. Then comes the dramatic courtroom scene in which Firoz pleads a memory lapse and does not offer evidence against

Maan Finally Man is compelled to leave Brahmpur in such unhappy spirits. His illicit relationship with Saeeda Bai ultimately pets his ruin and while be stakes his reputation and future for Saeeda Bai, she never marries him. A courtesan can never be accepted as a respectable daughter-in-law in Indian society. Seth does not restore what cannot be socially accepted in a convention-bound society and hence he may be said to take a very practical and realistic view of sex and marriage But Saeeda Bai cannot ever hope to regain her lost position. Her life is barren, as Susie Tharu explains that "to be public women was to be women who were not a private possession of the patriarch, a woman who did answer to the law of the father." (21)

Saeeda Bai's inner solitude, the meaninglessness of her glittering but caged life, the lack of emotional stability and her passing for a happy woman is another aspect of social life that forms the novel's pattern of contrast. The thematic significance of Saeeda Bai's life style is unmistakable, especially in bringing out the complexity of the novel. Saeeda Bai, empty of love and respect, says of the bareness of her life:

> "Now look at me....I still feel young..I am waiting to spend the evening with this disgustingly ugly man who is fifty-five years old, who picks his nose and belches, and who is going to be drunk even before he gets here. Then he'll want me to sing romantic songs for him...but what about my feelings?" (22)

Seth's deep comment on the social scene is well registered. The novel is built around the opposed concepts of domestic-life and marriage, on one hand, and sex life outside the home, on the other hand. Each concept becomes a kind of poetic intuition charged with emotional values. According to Seth, marriage is the symbol of peace and quiet, whereas sex outside marriage is the signal of misfortune, obscenity, irreligion and loneliness.

The role of women in the Indian society is also a thematic concern. In the India of 1950's, home was the only legitimate sphere of activity for women. There were mostly arranged marriages, with the result that the sole purpose of their education was to prepare them for matrimony und domestic drudgery. In the physical strength and intellectual capacity, they were supposed to be inferior to men. Delicacy and innocence were the main attributes of woman. However the younger generation of woman had started insisting on the equality of the sexes and condemning the conventional view which had reduced them to household drudges and commodities.

Seth portrays the world of past-independence women in detail. His women are associated with family clusters. He portrays a patriarchal world "where a visible-or invisible, yet no less effective-purdah shrouds the lot of women." (23) Male heads of famiily such as Mahesh Kapoor and the Nawab of Baitar celebrate the ideal domestic space as that where men and woman live within the specific roles delegated to them. They relegate their wives to a privatized domestic sphere having little or no impact on the 'public' sphere in which they themselves participate. The older women confirm to these patriarchal expectations of the wife, 'mother, and 'widow'. Married at sixteen and widowed at thirty seven, the helpless Mrs. Rupa Mehra was compelled to depend on the goodwill of others for support to allow her four children to continue to enjoy the benefits of an excellent English-medium boarding school education. Now in her mid forties, Mrs. Mehra preserves the memory of her deceased husband Raghubir Mehra, a senior civil servant, by the comic evocation of 'Him' in times of crises. Mrs. Mahesh Kapoor is the maternal pillar of support in Prem Nivas, the hopme of the Kapoor family. She is the "samdhin or the co-mother in law of both Mrs. Mehra and the old Mrs. Tondon.

The lives of Seth's younger women are also enmeshed within a domestic space." Lata reacts with indignation when she reads that married women are not eligible for jobs in either the Indian

Administrative Service or the Indian Police Service, and a woman might be required to resign from the service in the event of her marrying subsequently". (24) The narrative is emphatic towards women who have been denied opportunities. Veena Tondon faces still resistance from her mother-in-law when she wishes to pursue her passion for classical music. Priya Goel is S. S. Agarwal's daughter. She lives as a part of a joint family and is caught in an intolerable situation with her in-laws. Zainab is the Nawab's daughter, and another childhood friend of Veena. She disappears into the world of the purdah after her marriage and silently suffers the infedilities of her husband. The world of the zenana becomes Zainab's complete world. She crosses the geographical line that lay between the mardana and the women's space of the zanana, and displays great courage in order to save her ancestral Baitar House from the Custodian of Evacuee Properly. But having done so, she retreats back into an enclosure and remains on the periphery of the narrative. By describing restrictions enforced on woman, Seth does to some extent problematise the inherent spaces allowed to women by patriarchal discourses. He does not however invest them with agency to act or to other resistance. Although, Seth has touched upon oppression of the woman within the institution of the Indian marriage, but his main focus is still on the lengthy descriptions of happy domestic scenes between the "sweet tempered, fair complexioned, beautiful Savita" (Who is pregnant within a few months into her marriage) and Pran, "the first-class husband and son-in-law".

Nineteen years old Lata Mehra, the heroine of the novel, is a student of English literature at the University of Brahmpur and turns to Jane Austen on rail journeys, considers Tennyson as one of her favorite poets, and is also able to quote the poetry of Clough with amazing ease. "Lata is named after that most pitiable thing, a vine, which is trained to cling first to her family, then to her husband". (25) However she is not as pliable as her mother would have liked to believe. At her sister's wedding, she reflects on how Savita and Pran met just for an hour in her mother's company, and wonders if she would have agreed to be married of in such a summary manner. Descriptions of Lata comes to us from people around her, Kalpana Gaur is a close friend of the family, and describes her to Haresh Khanna as "attractive and smart in an Indian sort of way. She looks forward, I think, to a quiet, sober life in the future". (26)

The theme of denunciation of passions is thus established in the novel. Passion is shown as destructive, Maan's shattering experience of his mother's death results in a "violent revulsion of feeling" against himself, and against Saeeda Bai, for their passionate relationship. The overwhelming sense of guilt moves him into another world-beyond the reach of her attractions. Lata points out to Malati, "look at what passion has done to the family, Maan's broken, his mother's dead, his father's in despair. When 1 thought that Kabir was seeing someone else, what I remember feeling was enough to make me hate passion, passionately and forever". (27) To be so passionately involved was to be out of control like a boat heading for the rocks, and his could lead to emotional bankruptcy.

David Myers considers the passage on Lata's 'Pragmatic' denunciation of passion, and her explanation as to why she has renounced her romantic infatuation with Kabir, as pivotal for 'decoding' the decidedly moralistic slant that Seth has given to the climax. Myers reads Seth's stance as in opposition to "today's western craze for finding he elusive meaning of life through losing yourself in passion". (28). He continues:

> On the contrary to women's magazines which suggest that meaning of life is to be found in passionate romance, hi-fashion fame, and lust for the faster car, Seth suggests that it is to be found in arranged marriages, the renunciation of sexual demonism, and tolerant participation in the comic parliament of family

togetherness. Passion and fanaticism of all kinds must be dominant in the human personality if this family togetherness is to be the successful foundation of tolerance in national politics." (29)

The social realism in the novel is equally convincing. Calcutta is an apt choice for the setting of a cosmopolitan family like the Chatterjees, as Calcutta was the social, cultural, and political capital of the British in those days, long before Delhi became the centre of things. Seth recreates India of the 1950s for the reader piece by piece, reproducing University academics with its political rivalries and its dead end stagnation. The world of Mrs. Rupa Mehra, with all her maneuverings to find a suitable son-In-law, religious zeal outs who perpetrate riots, or scheming politicians who aid it them- especially the episode about raising or thee Shiva Lingam on the disputed site- all become relevant in light of the Ayodhya episode and the recent Gujarat violence. Seth brings the reader into the homes of the people who bear the impact of this religious frenzy. As the novel progresses, every aspect of Indian society is explored. In *A Suitable Boy*, then, the constant affirmations of tolerance must be understood not just as pertaining to State policies, but also as an ethical vision of a peaceful and humane society. Early in the text, Mahesh Kapoor, the Revenue Minister of the state of the Puva Pradesh, is established as Nehru's fictional counterpart, especially with respect to his views on religion and secularism. He operates as the local Nehruvian figure that is well known for his tolerance towards other religious and is liked and respected among the knowledgeable Muslims. Significantly, while Seth constitutes Mahesh Kapoor as a man who has due regards for other religious communities, he also indicts him as a patriarch who is intolerant of any kind of faith or belief. Much like Nehru, he is impatient with any form of religiousity. When his wife asks for his permission to organize a recital of the Ramcharitmanas in their house, he is dismissive of her feelings and says that he can't allow it in Prem Nivas as he has a secular mage. He further says that, he doesn't believe in the chanting and hypocrisy and fasting by saffron- clad heroes who want ban on cow slaughter and revive the Somnath temple and the Shiva temple and God knows what else. In a similar incident later in the text, Mrs. Mahesh Kapoor meets a like response when she seeks to perform shraadh for her husband's parents or watch the Ramlila. For Mahesh Kapoor, this is all mumbo- jumbo and idiocy. Thus although Seth persistently espouses Nehru's vision of a tolerant and secular India; he is not uncritical of the rationalist secularism of Mahesh Kapoor that demands emancipation from all forms of religious beliefs and practices.

The Raja of Marh lays the foundation stone of the temple -as a consequence, the Imam of the Alamgiri Mosque gives an inflammatory speech to his congregation on Friday, and in a typical instance of cyclical violence, a riot breaks out between the Hindus and Muslims of the city over clashing religious symbols. The call for prayer from the mosque is interrupted by the sound of conch. The characters themselves act charitably towards each other and the narration treats them warm- heartedly. The rhyme Savita writes in Lata s book advises both compassion and stoicism.

"Life is merely froth and bubble.

Two things stand like stone:

Kindness in another's trouble,

Courage in our own." (30)

In this spirit, Firoz forgives Maan and also tries to reconcile himself to his own father's youthful rape of Saeeda Bai. The Nawab Shahib, inspired by Firoz, also forgives Maan, and Firoz claims to have fallen on his own knife, thus getting Maan off charges of attempted murder. Characters are drown in the acceptance that people have idiosyncrasies and serious flaws- the important thing is not why they have them but how those around them will adapt to accommodate them.

Seth's critical eye also records realism which is one of the pervading aspect of *A Suitable*

Boy. According to Shyamala A. Narayan "Social realism is the keynote of *A Suitable Boy*. (31) Being written in the background of social, economic, political of newly Independent India, it deals with glorious and ore eventful period of Indian history. However, *The Telegraph* (11 September, 1993, 12) has pointed out, ***A Suitable Boy*** is singularly lacking in the other virtues of nineteenth century narrative realism such as the absolute ironic control of Austen, 'the mordant vein of Thackeray and the deep psychological insights into character and situation one's finds in Charles Dickens. (32)

However, I don't agree with *The Telegraph* because the indebtedness to the nineteenth century realists is clear enough, and is admitted within the novel itself. Amit Chatterjee, the Bengali poet and the suitor of Lata, who is in many ways mouthpiece of the author, at one point declares: "I still bear the scars of Middlemarch." Another suitor of Lata, Haresh reads the novels of Hardy, and in his drawing room "the volumes of Thomas Hardy on the small bookshelf were arranged alphabetically." (33)

Apart from the mention of the realists, Vikram Seth offers a blend of the fictional with actual historical characters and events. The main characters are invented, but the fictional politician Mahesh Kapoor, and his equally fictional Chief Minister S.S. Sharma, read a letter from the eminently real Jawaharlal Nehru-which, as Seth informs the readers in his prefatory notes, "reproduces word for word, parts of the letter actually sent by Nehru on 9th August 1951, to the Chief Ministers of u the Indian States." (34)

As a point of style and technique, it becomes evident that *A Suitable Boy* has been written with the leisureliness, the almost forgotten confidence of the Victorian novel. It is a throwback to an earlier generation when the art of novel-writing was an extension of reconteuring. Seth dons the mantle of omniscient author, but the authorial voice in *A Suitable Boy* is never conspicuous or overbearing. The novel is written with the quiet and unobtrusive style which Seth attributes to his own tastes and beliefs.

In this novel Seth's displays a taste tor scrupulous documentation. As a result, each major setting in the novel the weddings of Lata and Savita, the pul-mela, the raising of the Shiva-lingam, the religious festivities-is elaborately reproduced in its social and demographic entirety. Seth is in no hurry to wind up his saga and his unerring eye for detail leaves out nothing - he 1s not content merely with a page or two long description of Saeeda Bai sing-he must take the reader through the entire evening couplet by couplet, ghazal by ghazal. Every nuance, every gesture ("ada") is perfectly caught. For this reason *A Suitable Boy* can be a little hard on those readers who prefer fast paced novels. It is a novel strictly for those who are willing to be drawn, albeit temporarily, into world that Seth creates.

3.(E) Writing Style of A Suitable Boy

Seth's use of language in the novel is also unique, because *A Suitable Boy* is the only work in Seth's canon that occasions an examination of language. All Seth's other works employ flawless English, but with such an Indian subject, a tale written in unadulterated English would perhaps not have been so convincing, apart from being less apposite as well. India has adopted the English language for her own, blending it with every local dialect, so that It is no longer spoken as the Queen's English except by the elite. Consequently, the Indianism in *A Suitable Boy* is confined to middle class society. In such instances it becomes clear that the language being spoken is not English but Urdu, Hindi, or even Bengali, and Seth has provided a literal translation in order to preserve the idiom, without which the entire conversation would be lost. In the context of language it is noteworthy that Seth's passion for versification spills over into *A Suitable Boy*, with the academic connection through Pran and Lata, the weekly poetry sessions of the Brahmapur Literary Society, Amit's vacation, and the Chatterjee family's natural facility silly rhyme providing Seth with many opportunities indulge him.

Seth's style is so unique that the reader is irresistibly held by Seth's narrative technique, which is never heavy or dull, even when he is describing the drudgeries of Indian politics. The literary tradition Seth has inherited is essentially Western, and so the

Russian literary model adds *War and Peace* to *Eugene Onegin* and blends it with the Victorian model named in the novel itself- *Middlemarch*. Literary allusions are employed from Austen, E.M Forster, and like Eliot, Seth's use of pastiche enables him to intensify the character delineation.

Seth's style in this novel involves conjuring up a brilliant sense of the comic, evident especially when he writes about Chatterjees and their circle. The overwhelming atmosphere of the novel is one of tongue-in-cheek humor, despite the occasional dark storm clouds that gather. It is as if Seth is exhorting the reader to dwell on the comic aspects of everyday life rather than on the tragic ones, aware that reducing one's problems to the playful silliness of Kakoli-couplets will rob them of some of their gravity. Seth also seeks to divest the Indian Holy men and gurus of their mystic spirituality, presenting them as the majority of them really are opportunists. The swamis and the gullibility of their devotees provide some highly comic scenes in the novel. Yet, the happy spirit of the novel is neither sentiment nor blind, "it is a natural gift of the author, who never mocks or dismisses his characters."(35) Consequently, Seth's voice is not the voice of indignation but that of gentle and genteel comedy.

3.(F) Review of A Suitable Boy

Thus, it can be said that **A Suitable Boy** is a gigantic creation by Vikram Seth both massive and impressive. **A Suitable Boy** with its main theme of a search for a suitable groom for Mrs. Rupa Mehra's daughter Lata, and the innumerable other situations and projections involving four families, and the host of the people inhabiting those families, along with multiple moods, motives and a whole range of complex emotions; is one of the most fascinating creations in words in contemporary Indian Literature as a whole. **A Suitable Boy** is set wholly in India and the main strength of the novel lies not in the business of match making, but in the depiction of the social panorama of the decade after Independence. Seth manages to interlink in a credible way all the larger themes of political, social and religious conflicts, with day to day ordinary human emotions of his true-to life characters. A multitude of characters and events throng the novel , the setting moves back and forth between the cities of Brahmpur, which is fictional, and Calcuta (a world by itself), with excursions to New Delhi, Kanpur and Lucknow and to a remote village in the north, Debaria where Maan spends a month in exile. Seth offers a huge, thick, and multi-layered slice of Indian life that, in its veracity, serves to counter the widespread false views of India and improve the world's understanding of our country.

A novel gets the status of a literary classic, if the novelist gives appropriate style and expression through a language suited to it. Seth has done admirable work in presenting authentic characters, convincing situations permeating the rich network of the novel, through suitable language suiting different mindsets and conditions. Moreover, Seth is conscious of giving suitable sensibility to the particular novel and all in all he has proved himself as a great genius and presented himself a ideal for the young rising talents. Like a vast and huge blue sky over which is a part of an every eye Vikram Seth's novel rule the entire world and rests in the minds of all his reader.

Lastly, on other hand Seth charts a secular course as the only politically viable solution for a state like India, and on the other he presents a surprisingly traditional view of questions connecting to the private sphere, such as marriage, personal relationships, etc. He sees *A suitable Boy* as a plea for religious tolerance among other things. He says:

"It is an insult to Hinduism that these people have hijacked what it means to be Hindu....it's tolerance, understanding....not just trying to bash your neighbor over the head because he is Muslim. These things need to be said." (36)

A Suitable Boy is thus a novel with multiple themes. The central theme, the search for the suitable groom, carries with it all the other major and minor themes in an even handed and artistically linked fashion. Seth says, "This novel is linear partly because it is multi linear. There are several 'plots in it", and they help the main plot to stand upon firmer footing. Some of the themes look expanded at first glance but arc actually vehicles of Seth's meditations on life: and Seth's insights are usually very perceptive on human nature. Representing the society of a generation ago, Seth effortlessly rustles a variety of themes to take on India on the eve of her first general election, stopping to focus on every issue that might conceivably have a bearing on it. As the words of Ruth Morse, "*A Suitable Boy* is social satire and social history, from the politics of the great man to the maneuverings of a mother". (37) In spite of the novel's wrist spraining and purse-straining drawbacks, it has drawn world wide acclaim. Seth says that when the novel would show no signs of winding up, he would often tell himself. "There must be an audience for a tale cleanly told no matter how long it is." (38) He was right because in *A Suitable Boy*. Seth has created a world that will entice readers for decade s to come.

Refrences :-

1. A.K. Singh, "Vikram Seth's A Suitable Boy: A Critique," Indian Fiction of Nineties, ed. R.S. Pathak (New Delhi: Creative, 1997), p-11

2. John Bemrose, " Full–lotus Fiction- A Suitable Boy by Vikram Seth," MacLean Consumer Publication, Toronto, May 31, 1993

3. Seth Vikram "A Suitable Boy " Viking Penguin Ltd. 1993 :p-866

4. ibid p-1262

5. ibid p-32

6. ibid p-1159

7. A Suitable Boy p-686

8. A Suitable Boy p-167

9. A Suitable Boy p-184

10. A Suitable Boy p-196

11. Aijaz Ahmad, "Reading Arundhati Roy Politically", Frontline, Aug8, 1997 p-104-105

12. A Suitable Boy p- 128

13. A Suitable Boy p-251

14. A Suitable Boy p-245

15. A Suitable Boy p-1060

16. A Suitable Boy p-1075

17. ibid p-878-879

18. A Suitable Boy p-236

19. *A Suitable Boy p-46*

20. A Suitable Boy p-147

21. Susie Tharu *Articulating Gender*, (eds). Anjali Bhalande and Mala Pandurang Delhi: Pencraft International. 2000.)

22. A Suitable Boy p-119

23. Ali Lakhani, "A Suitable Boy", (Review). Rungh. Vol 2, No 1 & 2, 1993: p-57

24. A Suitable Boy p-458

25. A Suitable Boy p-22

26. *A Suitable Boy p-567*

27. A Suitable Boy p-1296

28. A Suitable Boy p-27

29. David Myers, Vikram Seth's Epic Renunciation of the Passions: Deconstructing Moral Codes in A Suitable Boy" Fiction of Nineties, (ed.) V.N Das and R.K Dhawan, prestige books: 1994 p-73

30. Seth Vikram, "A Suitable Boy" Viking Penguin Ltd. 1993: p-1150

31. Shyamala A. Narayan, "A Suitable Boy: An Exemplar of Artististic Freedom, The Quest, Vol. 8, No. 2, December 1994, p-10.

32. Sonba M. Salve, *The Novels of Vikram Seth: A Thematic and Stylistic Study*, Prestige Books International, New Delhi. P-86-87

33. A Suitable Boy p-573-74

34. *Christopher Rollason, " on Some Aspects of Language in Vikram Seth's A Suitable Boy," Atlantic Literary Review, Vol. 3, No 3, July-Septemper 2002, p-3*

35. Gupta Roopali, *Vikram Seth's Art: An Appraisal,* New Delhi: Atlantic Publishers and Distributors Ltd. P-68

36. Eugene Robinson, "A Tolstoy On His First Try" Washington Post. May 1, 1993.

37. Ruth Mores, Rooted Cosmopolite: Vikram Seth and "The Scars of Middlemarch". Fitzwilliam College, Cambridge,1994. URL: www.perso.worldonline.fr/ebe/s.html

38. Seth Vikram, "A Suitable Boy" Viking Penguin Ltd. 1993.

An Equal Music – A Study of Musical Techniques

4.(A) Introduction of An Equal Music

This chapter contains the central message of Vikram Seth's in *An Equal Music* to his readers. The writer celebrates the music of late eighteen century and early nineteenth century. Bach died in 1750 and Schubert in 1828, Mozart preceded them and Beethoven died just one year before Schubert. The musical range does not step outside these limits. The author has a fine knowledge of this music. The invocation of music as suggested in foregoing passages continues till the end of the novel. *An Equal Music* is the tale of an emotionally volatile musician, Michael Holme, and his gradual recovery of the self. The narrative deals with Michael's passionate relationship with his music; his deeply moving 12-year-old attachment to his 270-year-old Carlo-Tononi violin; and his intense love for a woman he loses twice over. It is about the resuscitation of a long dead love and the interaction of a group of musicians.

In *An Equal Music*, Seth makes an interesting point, his heroine Julia is deaf yet she pursues the career of a musician. Seth assumed the novel as a musical analogy, inspired by Bach, the famous musician in the eighteenth century, and his 'Art of Fugue'. Seth points out the deepening sense of frustration, helplessness of these musicians who have to perform according to their audience's choice and expectations in creating music that must essentially be enthralling soul stirring and which is able to outclass everything. Nevertheless, the audiences are oblivious and even unmindful of the tremendous pressure and the professional hazards involved in it. The novel delicately and evocatively describes their desire to perform and rise in their profession along with Julia's deafness who with the support of Michael finally finds her destination. Throughout the novel, music in its entire vicissitudes is projected. Symbolically it is the dream of all of them.

An Equal Music has been hailed as the finest novel about music ever written in English. Narrated in the present tense by Michael, the first hall of the novel is almost magical, with its melancholic evocations of London's Hyde Park, and its description of bracing Saturday- morning swims in filthy, freezing water of Serpentine. For Seth, writing about diverse themes and diverse places is a challenge and attraction n itself. This is a book about music and how the love of music can run like a passion through life. In the novel he creates a living, breathing world that enchants and grips the readers. It is about the resuscitation of a long dead love and the interaction of a group of musicians. Seth sought the help of friends as well us strangers, string players, composers, repairers and sellers of instruments all those who aid in dissemination of music. *An Equal Music* therefore, is music which has attained perfection and since music is the food of love, it plays a major role in a narrative of love lost and found and finally lost again. The book deals with perfect love, which is marked by balance, harmony, uniformity and tranquility. Seth's passion for music, his empathy with it and with the people who create and perform it, reflects through his book, making it totally different from anything else he has written.

Michael is a complex, somewhat temperamental young man whose birth place Rochdale, in the North of England, was once rich in orchestral and choral music. And, although music was never a part of his own parent's lives, at the age of nine, Michael was taken by Mrs. Formby to a performance of Handel's Messiah. It is here that he emerges himself in music and with borrowed instruments he takes a scholarship to the Royal Northern college of Music in Manchester, Later, he gets an invitation to join a master class at the Musikhochschule in Vienna, and amidst great opposition from his parents, he becomes a professional violinist. Music dominates both their lives, providing a counterpoint for every mood and action. And Seth keenly explores the strange dependence, and independence of the individuals involved in the Maggiore Quartet, the terrible dilemma of a musician who suffers almost total loss of hearing and the plight of musicians whose precarious income prevents them from ever owning the finest and the most beautiful of instruments and who, like Michael, may lose their much loved but borrowed instruments any time. The action moves between London, Vienna and Venice but the real life of the novel is the music- music equated with love and emotions. Michael is alone like he was in the beginning, but there is one important difference: his thoughts have reached a resolution and he is no longer troubled. He has learned acceptance and it has brought him serenity. This change in perspective has enabled him to come to terms with his past, made the present bearable, and the future promising. And perhaps most essentially of all, he has realized that to be complete is an advantage, not a necessity.

4.(B) Structure of An Equal Music

An Equal Music is a novel in which the length of Schubert's Trout Quintet matters deeply, the discovery of a little- known Beethoven Opus is a miracle, and each instrument has its own being. Just as Michael can't hope to possess Julia, he cannot even dream of owning his beloved Tononi, the violin he has long had only on loan. And it goes without saying that Vikratm Seth knows how to tell a tale, keeping us guessing about everything from what the quartet's four-minute encore will be to what really occasioned Julia's departure from Michael's life. On the other hand Julia explains that she is suffering from an autoimmune disease of the inner ear. This implies that the protective systems of her body are treating parts of the inner ear as hostile, and therefore destroying them. She is gradually going deaf with only lip-reading and hearing aids being her companions. But a time will come when the only music she will hear is the music in her mind. Julia has taught herself to watch the movements of other players and to play entirely from memory and imagination. She explains how her mental agony began three years ago and the tremendous support given to her by her husband James, who encouraged her to play again as music is the heart of her life. Michael gets a book on deafness to understand Julia's problem better.

Seth assumed the novel as a musical analogy by Bach, the famous musician in eighteenth century, and his 'Art of Fugue'. 'The Art of Fugue, is essentially violent and vibrant, going on between the centripetal and centrifugal forces. Seth's Western Classical musicians are a part or a quartet comprising a viola player, a cellist, and two violin players.

Michael, the main protagonist in the novel, is one of the violinists. At the opening of the novel Michael is seen bereaved, wretched and listless. Nothing excites him and the sudden parting from Julia, his beloved only enhances the existing loneliness. It has been ten years since Julia and he parted, while at the moment, he was going along with a student, Virginie. There was only lust and no love involved in their relationship. This shows the western Civilization as Michael, thirty Seven years old indulges with her, who is barely sixteen. Michael is middle aged and the everyday struggle for a humble life style hardly allows him to think about a life partner or anything required for a settled life. The dreary life moves on; it is devoid of zest and focus. Michael undoubtedly is trying to assuage his loneliness through sexual gratification with someone he does not love.

An Equal Music is as much a novel about love and music as about a certain inner darkness. It has a melancholic strain that manifests itself in the isolation of the characters, in Michael's obsessions, Julia's deafness, in the lack of common perspectives, even the humour is dark, serving chiefly to make the tragic parts more poignant by contrast, along with the goal of providing "dramatic relief', to borrow a term from Shakespearean criticism, as the story grows almost suffocatingly sad. There are some brief glances towards colonizing areas in the novel. His authorial note at the close of *An Equal Music* is the only acknowledgment that his appropriation of the great aesthetic tradition of Western Classical music is his entry into zones of contact, or harnessing cultures that have despite many movements to and fro largely retained their Eurocentric locations. The novel is Eurocentic to its musical Core and each aspect of it such as plot, characterization, and theme bespeaks of an authority consciousness that is completely in control of the narrative it commands and constructs. Furthermore, the control of the idioms and nuances of an elite European culture is not limited to the cast of characters and their behavior pattern, even their emotional grid is mapped within a discourse that is culturally specific. At this point one may pause and say that Seth, as a creative artist, has complete license to appropriate the areas he does and mould them in ways that suit his sense of novelist design.

The novel moves to an end with its Keatsian acceptance of the inexorable cycle of nature. "Nothing stops. The Hawthorn is green in berry, psycaranthe ripe. This newfound maturity burgeons to include the chastening acknowledgement of life's processes ending in death. Carl Kall, Michael's music teacher is pictured as dying on a 'cold blue-skied day." (1) When Julia closes the door on Michael's face finally and deliberately, he knows how he must take it though it will still take him, some more time to completely accept it. Once again, it is significant that this ultimate edification comes through the agency of nature:

"A Small dog sits on
the sneezing prow. Go, then,
with the

breathing tide, and do
not make a scene, and learn
wisdom of the little

dog, who visits from
elsewhere, and who knows
that what it is, is, and O

harder knowledge that

what is not is not." (2)

An Equal Music focuses on music and passion, draped in European settings. Much of the story takes place in London, though Vienna and Venice become central as well. Through the eyes of the Musicians, the reader sees these tours as holy pilgrimages. The novel resonates with Seth's precise details from the musical history of the cities to the large Campri sign on the isle of Lido, across Vienna from Venice to London. The novel examines the impact of Western classical Music on the lives and hopes and fears and finally, desperate choices of its European protagonists. As viewed by Anjana Sharma Seth's novel was stunning by many accounts, not the least of which was its grafting of the twin bulwark of the European tradition-its verbal and aural inscriptions onto the life of its thirty something protagonists suggest. She further viewed, "Seth tells the story of a young man's growth and maturation-the loss and partial recovery, Pip-like, of his lost love, and the loss, and more certain recovery of his artistic self". (3)

Seth's passion for music, his empathy with it and with the people who create and perform it, reflects through this book, making it totally different from anything else he has written. Michael is a complex, somewhat temperamental young man whose birthplace Rochdale, in the North of England, was once rich in orchestral and choral music. And, although music was never a part of his own parent's lives, at the age of nine, Michael was taken by Mrs. Fromby to a performance of Handel's Messiah. "More than anything else", he reflects, "I wanted to be a part of that noise." So, he immerses himself in music and with borrowed instruments he takes a scholarship to the Royal Northern College of Music in Manchester. Later he gets an invitation to join a master-class at the Musikhochschule in Vienna, and amidst great opposition from his parents, he becomes a professional violinist.

On this premise Seth bases *An Equal Music*, comprehending that writing about an artist is incomplete without exploring the intricacies of his art. In this exploration Seth's genius shines through: in making accessible to the reader the lifelong immersion in and maintenance of a craft that is the foundation of all serious music making. As one character admits, "This morning I suddenly realized how boring musicians are. All our friends are musicians and we aren't interested in anything except music." (4)

Seth uses the four members of the Maggiore to depict how difficult and complicated the life of a dedicated quartet can be. Piers, a member of the quartet, says:

> "It's the weirdest thing, a quartet. I don't know what to compare it to. A marriage? a firm? a platoon under to self-regarding, self-destructive priesthood? It has so many different tensions mixed in with is pleasures." (5)

We learn Michael's story gradually as he goes about his daily routines of teaching, solitary practice and rehearsal, until he gets a fleeting glimpse ofJulia - on a passing bus - whom he had once loved and left in Vienna and has been unable to find again since. The search for Julia, their meeting and its consequences, are woven into other larger themes. Music dominates both their lives, providing a counterpoint for every mood and action. And Seth keenly explores the strange dependence, and independence of the individuals involved in the Maggiore Quartet; the terrible dilemma of a musician who suffers almost total loss of hearing; and the plight of musicians whose precarious income prevents them from ever owning the finest and the most beautiful of instruments and who, like Michael, may lose their much loved but borrowed instruments at any time.

The novel's concentration on an elite circle of musicians, playing elite music for people like them might be deemed pretentious but for several important factors. For one there is Michael, Seth's first person narrator and the quartet's second violinist. Michael is to some extent an outsider. He is not a Londoner by birth, nor is he of a musical background. He grew up in Rochdale, the son of a small businessman and has had to work against his parents' prejudice as well as that of the more privileged people he encounters in musical circles. His confidence in himself and his abilities is always undercut by his sense that he doesn't quite belong, as well as his knowledge that nor does he fit in back in Rochdale either. This sense of displacement echoes back to the themes Seth explored in *A Suitable Boy*, albeit in a very different way.

The fragility of Michael's situation is symbolized by two very important figures. One of them is his Tononi violin, which is owned, ironically enough, by a Rochdale connection, the wonderful Mrs. Formby. The other is Julia McNicoll, who Michael abandoned when they were both music students in Vienna. Much of the narrative is concerned with Michael's perception of these two relationships and the parallels between them. It soon becomes apparent that Michael's feelings of tenderness and his fear of loss are bound up with both Julia and the Tononi. In addition, Julia is not merely a cipher for Michael's frustrated passion, but a character in her own right, with a secret that threatens to throw her and everyone around her completely off their axis.

Another factor which keeps the narrative grounded is the presence of humour. Much of this concerns Piers, the quartet's brilliant, very intense first violinist. Piers has the habit of getting into very deep relationships with unsuitable men. His romances throw the dynamics of the quartet completely off-balance and make him impossible to live or work with. He is also, amusingly, protective of certain works, for example Schubert's Trout Quintet. Those who are not fond of the Trout (as I am not) will find Pier's fixation with it even funnier than his poor taste in men.

An Equal Music published in 1999 received considerable attention and interest from literary critics and academicians as his previous novels *The Golden Gate* and *A Suitable Boy* established him as a writer par excellence. **An Equal Music** as the title suggests is a story of love and loss set against the background of music. It is a novel of moderate size consisting 381 pages as compared to the epic dimensions of the previous novel, *A Suitable*

Boy. "***An Equal Music*** is a tale of an emotionally volatile musician. Seth explains that the idea of writing a novel about a musician took its roots from a visual image of a musician. Walking across a park on a very wet day, Seth and his companion Philippe Honore see someone staring at his own image in the water of the serpentine river in Hyde Park. As they wonder about the man, Philippe suggested that he might be a musician, and thereby the idea for the novel took root." (6). Seth dedicates the book **An Equal Music** to his friend Philippe Honore, as the idea occurred to him in the companionship of this man. The novel is story of a musician, Micheal Holden and his emotional attachment to Julia and his violin. Vikram Seth has succeeded in creating a living, breathing world of music and the narrative enchants and grips the reader. Seth remarks at the end of the novel, in the author's note: "Music to me is deeper than speech. When I realized that I would be writing about it, I was gripped with anxiety. Only slowly did I reconcile myself to the thought of it." Even in his earlier books, Seth refers to the theme of music. In ***The Golden Gate***, there are references to both pop and western classical music. In ***A Suitable***

Boy also, he talks about the ragas and the ghazal performances by Saeeda Begum. Seth himself studied the khayal under Pandit Amarnath during his short visits to India. The classical Indian music and the vocal music influenced him in writing about music in his novel.

4.(C) Themes of An Equal Music

In ***An Equal Music*** Seth adopts the first person narrative mode, in contrast to the omniscient mode that he adopted in the earlier novels. Seth explains why he chose to write in this mode. Firstly he understood that it was "notoriously difficult" to write about an acceptable art form in an expository way, and therefore the only way to get into music through words was to describe the thoughts of someone actually a musician himself. Secondly, an idea of telling an intense love story in the first person held a greater appeal to him. The device of the narrative helps the author to view the world of music from the eye of a musician. It is the voice of the protagonist. There is a distance and nearness to the writer. As a tale of intense and passionate love, the voice of the person who has experienced the joy and agony of love suits the purpose. As the hero himself is narrating, the issue of authenticity of feeling does not enter the mind of the reader at any point. His narration gives voice to his agony and his passionately imaginative mind paved the way to his emotions. It is only by surrounding himself in the emotional extravagance of sensations, he could play at all. He is thirty-seven year old and is a second violinist in an English quartet, named Maggiore. Michael also teaches violin to a few music students. The reader enters into the world of Michael's life from the daily routines of teaching, solitary practices and rehearsals and his getting the fleeting glimpse of Julia, whom he had loved and lost in Vienna and has been unable to find again. Michael's search for Julia, their meetings and parting are all woven in the story. At the same, the story of other musicians of the quartet, Maggiore has also been given space. The plight of the musicians whose precarious income prevents them from buying the finest and most beautiful instrument of their choice and requirement is also portrayed in the novel. The reader is also thrown into the lives, whims and chemistries of classical musicians.

The socio-cultural concept combines two main fields: society and culture. Community involves a group of people who are the members of various societies, and culture is the conduct of the community as a whole. Social-cultural viewpoints represent the psychology, economics, gender, ethnicity, political, structure, religion, practice, custom, belief and values of the particular society. The book portrays European's socio-cultural experiences and the immigrants' struggle to adopt it. Michael states:

> " I get through the
> rehearsal a day passes,
> then another. I buy bread
> and milk. I eat, drink and
> bathe, I shave. Exhausted
> by wakefulness, I sleep. I
> teach. I attend rehearsals.
> I turn on the news and
> absorb the words. I
> exchange greetings with
> our porter and the other
> denizens' of our building.
> As once before, after I

fled Vienna, My brain
and   body   direct
themselves." (7)

Such European performers, musicians, singers all move very swiftly from one location to another in order to practice and perform well. But wherever they go, the characters never neglect their religious get-together, festivals and celebration. Virginie one of the musicians in the Michael troop decides to go Nyons her native place to celebrate Christmas with her family. However, Virginie the young artist is very busy in her professional field; she wants to take part in her family cultural activities. This represented their culture.

The second part of the novel describes how the music functions as a perfect remedy for the people who are internally affected. Music is an unsurpassable thing and it plays a major role in the culture. Michael separates from Julia and he bares the pain only with the help of music. The third part of the novel describes the picture gallery, which represents the artists and their culture. Michael and Julia go to the picture gallery, they amaze to see it, and naturally, they come out of their stress and pain. The life of the artists, musicians, and singers seem to be interesting because they visit many places and see various cultures. However, their personal life is not enjoyable as they always give pleasure to the audience through their eternal music.

Vikram Seth depicts his characters along with their culture, tradition, and celebrations. This book describes how the young people are interested to celebrate the religious ceremony. Nicholas Spare, a music critique, invited Michael to a musician's pre-Christmas party. Michael's co-musicians like Erica Cowan, Nicholas, and Piers discussed a modern music, opera at the party amongst themselves. Mr and Mrs. Farmby observed the spiritual event so they explore locations such as Rochdale, Middletons, Bolton, and Cheshire and celebrate the spiritual ceremonies there. These cultural travelers travel to the various places, play their music, and spread their culture. All the old and new performers met together in the Wighmore Hall to rejoice.

Vikram Seth explains Michael's and Julia's miserable and lonely lives. While Michael wanted to live with Julia, Julia who did not like Nora in <u>A Dolls House</u> wants to severe the familial connection. Julia still keeps up with her culture and adheres to her limitations, though she is a modern woman. Michael decided to leave Vienna forever in his frustration:

"Beloved
Schubert, in your city
I am adrift. I am
consumed by past
love; its germs long
embedded,   half
contained,   have
grown more virulent
again. There is no
hope for me. I turned
away four thousand
nights ago, and the
path was closed it by
trees and brambles. I
am eaten by futile
pity. I make too much
of much… How can I

long for what I do not
grasp?" (8)

The lovers did not cross the principles of culture. The marital life of Julia awakes her to behave in a proper manner. The life of Michael was very disturbed because of the separation. However, Michael and Julia are usually bound in this situation, their culture would not allow them to behave like lovers. This explains the significance of the bond of familial life. He tells him:

> "Though we are
> alone, we do not kiss; we
> are almost shy. The
> journey is everything it
> could be. The day grows
> warm, and I am like a
> torpid bee. Soon we are
> in the Veneto… The two
> of us stand in the
> corridor with our
> luggage and look out
> over the water. I speak
> her name softly to

myself,   and   she,
somehow sensing it or is
it   chance?   -   Speaks
mine." (9)

Unfortunately, Julia has lost her hearing capacity, but the deaf from childhood can easily get instructions because they are trained. Julia is not associated with signs and symbols used by the deaf since she is born with all physical abilities. However, she learned all the aspects she needed to understand her events. Her passion for music allows her to feel the world of music. Julia behaves like a born deaf because she very easily adopts the silent notes of the music.

Musicians,   artists,   and   singers   are transmitting their culture across the borders of their nations. Michael plays his violin to get out of his anger, whenever he feels frustrated. It's perfection beyond simple, perfect and inexorable imagination. Vikram Seth therefore concentrates on music that created gladness. In some ways, Vikram Seth presented a cultural dispute. Even if they belong to different nations and cultural backgrounds, all musicians, singers, and artists live together in a different society and culture in another country. All the musicians wander around and perform their art in different countries, but they attach themselves to their original culture and social life.

Writing letters to the dear ones was very important habit in those days. Through retrospective narrative skill, Seth links the current and the past. He often uses letters to express the memories of characters from his life as an effective means. Michael gets a letter from his old Viennese teacher and the letters by Michael to Julia to express his love and affection. The letters describe the inner nature of the characters. The culture of the sending letters is diminishing today. Through letters, one can express their feelings and expressions in a very transparent manner. And, those who read the old letters sent by their loved one's recollected all the past memories.

Unlike **The Golden Gate**, which looked at a specific defining moment in contemporary American culture, there is no distancing of the writer from the host society in **An Equal Music**. Interestingly **An Equal Music** has been received much more positively in India, than did *A Suitable Boy*. Almost all the newspaper were vehement in their criticism of the Booker people when it was learnt that *An Equal Music* did not figure in the final list of short-listed writers; "... where would Vikram Seth figure in this scheme of things. *An Equal Music* with its poignant love story between Michael and Julia set against London and Austria hardly throws open a colonial wonderland. So what if critics have hailed it as "wonder work: irresistible, tense, deeply moving". (10)

The protagonist, Michael drenched in love and longing narrates the story of his past and present in the voice of a broken hearted lover. In the story of this passionate love music plays an important role. The lines of the narrator and even other characters have music in them. As compared to the narrative techniques of the earlier novels, *An Equal Music* is different. The voice of the author in previous works provided Seth an opportunity to display his wit, humor, satire and gentle mocking of the characters, whereas in *An Equal Music*, as the hero he is narrating the events, this quality of wit and humor is lacking. However, the device of the first person narrative has enabled the writer to explore and expand the theme from the point of view of a musician. John Carry suggests that Donne's phrase of leave taking yields apt meaning as it brings out the balance between the four instruments that the quartet aims at, and the sound of unheard music in Julia's head matching the sound of her playing. Donne is speaking of an equal music as a metaphor for perfect peace, harmony and balance to be attained in the heavenly realm. Seth in the novel ***An Equal Music*** presents the story of Micheal's love for music, his love and loss of his lady love Julia and his attachment for Tonani, his violin. However the separation from his favorite violin does not take place, as Mrs. Form by, a true lover of music leaves this valuable instrument in the right hands.

Seth imparts an authentic picture of the Western classical musicians along with the insipidness and uncertainty in their lives, in spite of note being a part of it. The quartet players, accustomed to the torn and strife, disagreements and disputes, become the focal issue in the story. The four players have their own likes and dislikes.

Vikram Seth has maintained stability in the relationships also. It is seen that Julia feels guilty about her acts of deception. She cannot reconcile to living in a dual world which chafes each other. She admits to her intense love for Michael but decides to forgo her love for her husband and son. Michael is her past, and she realizes that one cannot live in the past forever. And she finally ends her relationship with Michael. Her choice to opt for her dependable (though unmusical) businessman- husband James over the volatile and moody Michael and her denunciation of passion for family and social order is one of the thematic preoccupations. Julia chose the stable and dependable James rather than Michael. For Julia, James had stood by her in the worst days when she could hardly recognize herself in the mirror; she saw in his eyes her existence. But in Michael's presence, she becomes restless and uncertain, afraid and guilty. Seth has presented two types of stability in the novel, social and the familial one, and the other mental and internal one. Also stressed again and again is the fact that attachment to love and music also leads to a sense of order and stability though of a different type, and *An Equal Music*, in spite of the individual's sense of loneliness, suggests that.

In *An Equal Music*, Seth takes a conventional romantic plot one renders it new and compelling through the attractive clarity and precision of its prose. One of the most impressive aspects of this novel is the way which it manages to convey music through Michael's daily drama and battles as a member of a quartet. The reader is thrown into the lives, whims and chemistries of classical musicians. In the book there are several moments when intense discussions on Schumann and Bach become too tedious for us commoners. The novel has a unique flavor- a strange pungent mingling of wild romance and domestic realism, of cosmic music and local details. The two chief characters are drawn with an unforgettable poetic intensity. *An Equal Music* links an exciting and romantic story to a sober and honest realism- a tragic story that ends with an Aristotelian catharsis for all the players in the drama.

The title of the novel ***An Equal Music*** is taken from an apt sermon by Donne, epigraphed to the novel, the sermon reads: And into that gate they shall enter, and in that haouse they shall dwell, where there shall be no cloud or sun, no darkness nor dazzling, but one equal light, no noise nor silence, but one equal music, no fears nor hopes but one equal possession, no foes nor friends, but one equal communion and identity, no ends or beginnings, but one equal eternity. Here "equal" becomes a synonym for the divine, for something that is perfect beyond imagining. The epigraph from John Donne with which the novel begins and from which the title is taken has the word 'equal' repeated five times: "one equal light", "one equal music", one equal possession", "one equal communion and identity", "one equal eternity". Setting the tone for music of the novel this sense of equanimity or harmony is used as a major trope, appearing as harmonious groups or groups which aspire toward harmony, in the musical aspirations of characters, or in relationships between individuals.

The title fits in very well with the spirit of the novel: the music of the masters is an equal music to Michael's ears, for it enables him to temporarily touch this divinity and gives his soul sustenance to go on. And not only is the music an equal one, but the love, as envisioned by Seth, grows into an Equal, perfect love, marked by balance and equability, understanding and acceptance. The novel thus reiterates Seth's earlier philosophy of the value of such mundane institutions as home and family.

An Equal Music is the story of Michael Holme, narrated by him. He is a second violin player in the moderately successful Maggiore Quartet. His is a story of music, of relationships that make music, and of the hard-won harmonies that make life worth living. It is a tear- jerking love story. Michael loves Julia. Not realizing how much he loves her, Michael leaves Julia. He rediscovers her ten years later; by which time she is married with a child and, tragically (because she is a pianist) going deaf. Their brief reunion serves to prove the impossibility of their romance, but at the same time the failure of romance enables Michael to think beyond himself, contemplating a larger reason for being. The novel deals with the variations on the theme of love. The analysis identifies the nature of the movement of the protagonist Michael Holme. Though the focus is on Michael, one can also identity this growth in the heroine Julia McNicholl. There are three phases in the life of Michael when he moves from imaginary to symbolic order. In the case of Julia we find two phases.

The story is about Michael Holme the butcher's son from Rochdale, who pursues the career of a musician. He is supported by a wealthy widow Mrs. Formby who lends her violin to him. He studies music under the famous teacher Professor Carl Kall in Vienna. In this city he falls passionately in love with Julia McNicholl who is keen to become a concert pianist. Michael starts having tensions with his teacher and finds the atmosphere very oppressive. He nearly reaches a point or nervous breakdown and leaves his place abruptly. Julha who had tried to convince him to face it all bravely, is shattered by this strange act of Michael. Even Carl Kall who had expected a bright career from Michael- his favourite student-is deeply hurt. When Michael returns to normal life and tries to contact Julia, he finds that her doors are closed to him.

Michael settles down in London and Joins Maggiore Quartet as second violinist and does manage to attain some fame as a musician. But he is never able to forget Julia. Chance brings them together after ten years. Both are unable to resist the power of their past and the relationship is revived. For sometime everything seems to be golden. Julia accompanies the Maggiore Quartet as a pianist to Vienna and Venice. However, Julia's marriage and her tragic hearing lost again pose a problem in their relationship. Julia ultimately decides to leave Michael and live a stable life with her husband and son. Michael is once again lonely. The only silver lining is the tie of the music. He listens to Julia's concert performance as a deaf pianist and is enthralled by the music. The novel ends on a tragic note. Now it is easy to understand the analysis of Michael s movement or growth as an artist from an imaginary to the symbolic order. The first phase of Michael's life as a child, especially at the age of nine, is one of the imaginary orders.

Michael's father was a butcher and his mother, too, didn't have any inclination for music. So, though the symbolic order was totally unsuitable to young Michael, yet the presence of the generous Mrs. Formby supplied the imaginary state of happiness. His father wanted him to study in a university and pursue a career in traditional kind of subjects. Even his mother had felt that Rochdale offered nothing and the only way to escape from this constrained town was to go to a university. His parents had sacrificed a lot to provide him education. They also felt that Michael won't be able to support a family. He was even said that they cannot provide him money for the violin and other expenses. But Michael faces the situation bravely. The symbolic order is traditional and the social world is hard. He decides to borrow Mrs. Formby's violin and do some jobs to support him. This decision of Michael creates a rift between him and his father. His mother too dies. With great difficulty, Michael bears the state of symbolic order, does manage to earn so that he can live in

Manchester and finally gets to convince his father that he was right to a great extent in deciding to become a musician. So, Michael standing firm and elevated has a remarkable growth in his personality- from a butcher's son to a musician of some reputation.

In comparison to Michael, Julia undergoes the process of movement from the imaginary to the symbolic order. She experiences it twice in her life. She hails from a background that provides her the ideal state or imaginary order. Even her life in Vienna is a continuation in imaginary order. She enters the symbolic order when Michael leaves Vienna. The ideal world crashes. But, she encounters the symbolic order courageously and settles down to a routine life with James, a businessman and their son Luke. However the worst is still to follow. She starts having hearing loss. This deficiency is really unbearable for many, what to say of a musician for whom sound matters so much. She prepares herself for the deafness with her husband's support and restricts her ambition as a concert pianist.

The imaginary order enters her life for a second time tor a very brief period when she meets Michael and their relationship is revived. It is a world of love and music once again. But, the reality of the symbolic order intrudes soon. She has her duty towards her family and her deafness is increasing day by day. She decides finally to repress her feelings of love and settle down to a life of security with her husband and son. She knows that past cannot be lived again. Even with total deafness in her life, she gives beautiful music to the world. Not only has she lived accepting pain of the love lost but also her permanent deficiency of hearing. Indeed she is victorious because has still so much to give to the world and add beauty to it.

Michael on the other hand takes a long time to calm down. As usual, he cannot accept the symbolic order. But this time he cannot emerge successful- trying to convince his father and teacher that he has carved a niche for himself after all. He cannot play music when he learns Julia will play 'The Art of Fugue'. This causes a break with the Maggiore Quartet. His violin too is nearly taken away. He even contemplates suicide but manages to come out of depression. He goes to a prostitute and even plays music for cheap ads. He is on the verge of a nervous breakdown. Mrs. Formby's death enables Michael to keep the violin. This kind gesture on her part ultimately saves Michael. A very slow, imperceptible process of healing starts. He meets Piers in a party. Piers requests him to return to Maggiore Quartet.

Michael had decided to do away with memories of Julia and not to attend her concert. But, he cannot help himself. He attends her concert and once again her music uplifts him. Seth's concluding lines of *An Equal Music* confirm Michael's healthy acceptance of the symbolic order:

> "Music, such,
> is a sufficient gift. Why ask
> for happiness, why hope not
> to grieve? It is to be blessed
> enough, to live from day to
> day and to hear such music-
> not too much, or the soul
> could not sustain it from time
> to time". (11)

Music and love are the two major themes in the novel, which is appropriate, considering that both love and music play on the emotions. It is interesting how Seth weaves the two together to create a canvas on which the passions are so consummately depicted- obsessive love; lives spent trying to recapture perfection. For the two principles- Michael and Julia, music is not merely a vocation, it is their avocation, and it has the strength to tie them to each other beyond the boundaries dictated by social norms, because their love has their music-making as its foundation. For Michael, Julia is not only the love of a life time; she is the very essence of his craft. This is why their love, though evident enough on the purely physical level, vibrates with a touch of transcendence that elevates them above anything sordid and contrives to keep them innocent somehow. Julia in spite of her conflicting loyalties is as powerless as is Michael to resist sinking into the tangled beauty or their love.

But Michael's and Julia's is not the only the relationship in the novel. The love between humans and music, instruments, dead composers, even the cities in which their music is played are very interesting that is why music usurps love's place as central theme. The characters not only love each other for the music they make, but also their passion for and their devotion to their music outlasts their travails and escapades by far. An elderly woman's love for music gives a small town boy his profession and ultimately, the cherished Tononi violin. Michael's relationship with his violin has been realized with a rare insight, not only Michael, but also all the other musicians empathize majorly with their respective instruments. The unspoken words that surged up in his mind were these:

> "I love it |the violin) and it loves me. We have grown to love each other. How can a stranger hold and sound what has been in my hands so long? We have been together for twelve years. Its sound is my sound. I can't bear to part with it." (12)

Thus, the love between instruments is also considered as one of the supreme points in the novel. In the world of music to which Michael belongs, there are such ascending and descending scales, sometimes sharply rising and then ebbing swiftly; personal loss and gain become irrelevant within the lovely, vigorous world of music. It was one such vigorous orchestral concert in which Michael and his group played Bach's 'Art of Fugue's, which brought Julia to Michael again. It was played with such intensity, such calm, as could not be imagined earlier. While the Orchestra was going on, Michael received a note that he had turned his lowest string down a tone in order to be able to play it. He did it though it was a source or anxiety to him. The experiences of playing together again and of making love elevate Michael to the height of ecstasy.

Music and love are thus equated finally, implying an end of all anxieties and a peace of mind. Perfect music and perfect love belong to the ideal world and man has to be content with glimpses of the ideal. Michael learns this lesson after he has undergone lots of tensions and anxieties. Sometimes he has almost collapsed out of sorrow, on some occasions, anger and jealousy gets the better of other emotions; occasionally, again, he lapses into self-pity. 1he effect of the novel is thus, like the effect of music that is composed out of a perfect blending of high pitched tones which are woven together into a whole. Being alert about the form, Vikram Seth delineates the nuances of the characters mostly through their expressions. All the characters contribute to the specific tone required by the novel. Piers is a natural musician, much disciplined but not rigid. A homosexual, Piers tries to run a tight ship. Billy is soft with hard centre. Once he gets some idea into his head, it is difficult to dislodge it. Always late for everything, Billy prefers to rehearse than to perform. It is Billy who gives his ticket to Michael, as he has felt that Michael must see the performance by Julia. Helen is a wonderful player who is merged in music. Through the gestures shown by Helen when she feels that Michael is undergoing emotional troubles, Vikram Seth is able to draw her sketch, brief and clear. The minor characters too, are tuned in the unique form. Vikram Seth's crafty depiction of characters, often through brilliant and witty conversations, charged with pathos, irony and humour, helps to make the structure of the novel perfect.

Seth brings in Tennyson's immortal lines to reveal that though Michael has been unfortunate in love, he has to come out of his self-pity and indulge in higher goals. The realization of the secret is behind true happiness dawns on him that it lies more in giving than in getting. Besides, the novelist also depicts the relevance and significance of such great sayings which never become obsolete. In the novel there is a glimpse of disobedience and unemotional attitude in the character of the protagonist, Michael Holme. He is seen selfish sometimes in the novel. Firstly, his insane behaviour towards his teacher shows the disobedience; secondly, his parents who sacrificed a lot to provide him education never wanted him to opt his career as a musician. They also felt that he would not be able to support family. It is not that he never bothered about his parents but his interest towards music was more powerful than any other thing which he can even think of. He can be very well said as a careless person. Against his parents wish he decided to be a musician which indicates somewhat unsentimental and unemotional look in his personality. He neither became a good child to his parents nor an obedient student to his teacher. Moreover, leaving Julia behind without informing his own immediate departure from the Maggoire Quartet and Vienna on account of a quarrel with his teacher, not to respond even after, any letters, no information shows Michael's careless behavior. His illicit relation with his student Virginia shows his selfishness. He could have proved a good teacher but he doesn't have any specific character. As if it was the time which takes decisions in his life.

> "The branches
> are bare, the sky tonight a
> milky violet. It is not quiet
> here, but it is peaceful. The
> wind ruffles the black
> water….. There is no one
> about. The birds are still."
> (13)

In a novel that begins with this kind of a lyrical description or a natural setting, the extensive role allotted to nature in the rest of the book comes as quite an acceptable follow-up. Deploying it in both traditional and non-conventional ways, Seth is able to infuse variety and depth into a novel which is otherwise located in the insular worlds of music and love. Even a first quick reading of the book will transport the reader to the midst of the relationship between characters and nature. In fact, this is one of the means of characters categorization that Seth uses. Michael, the musician protagonist of the novel shares a special bond with nature and makes it abundantly clears in his repeated avowals. He chooses his flat in central London for the view of nature from his window. He exults that he loves the view, his window looks down on brown-branched Hyde Park, one of his favorite walks is through the Park by waters of Serpentine, and he loves the query luxury of swimming in the open air in the hear of London.

Julia's craving for music is fulfilled which gives her the right direction as well as a good diversion from deepening sense self-pity. Such is the power of real music that it gives an inner beauty and strength to Julia that overpowers her physical handicap and she in turn is able to give pleasure and succour to thousands of weary minds and souls. Michael is determined to give strength to Julia and finally he succeeds. In a four minute section Julia performs exquisitely and Michael is driven to a sense of 'equal music'. The satisfaction he gets out of it is unequalled; there is no more any regret of losing Julia. He is moved to a sense of that equal music which Donne had expressed and which Seth borrowed for the epigraph. The verse achieves the end that a fugal composition presupposes, the composition that ultimately unites with the divine. The peace and tranquility that the artists obtain is such that they are unfazed by any kind of darkness or pain and will sustain them as long as they live. Nature is one of themes which is lingering in the novel. It is worth noting that this narrative about the disquieting lost love of a luckless English musician, Michael Holme, opens, thus: the vacant space left by Julia, is always located in an 'anti-nature position. She is never quite in synchrony with nature. Hence, she is characterized by her lack of relationship with nature, always as seen in the context of machines like her car. She is quite decidedly in opposition to nature.

She reacts disgustedly to his robust involvement in the activities of water serpents, the freaky group which revels in swimming in the murky waters of Serpentine, however full of "rat- piss and goose-turds' it might be. Wrinkling her nose up against the filthy freezing water." (14) She vociferously asserts that there is absolutely no way in which she can understand what is that attracts him and binds him with the open air.

Seth also acknowledges the crucial importance to the psychic journey which has manifestations in physical journey of his hero. *An Equal Music* concludes with Julia's concert at the Wigmore Hall. Michael goes to attend it, takes away with him the impregnable impression of the sound of music. The novel is full of musical majestic discoveries and revelations. Seth carries out the story line of "*An Equal Music* with great lucidity, tact and decorum, it echoes the view that a novel is more a way of travelling than apoint of arrival, more an invitation to wander than a secure niche, and more akin to the way a man enters and meanders through this world than to reach an assumed resting place in the afterlife." (15) Moreover, in a novel in which memory has an important role to play, the effort to recall the wonderful yet hopeless relationship of love is also located integrally in the heart of the picture of this idyllic yet confounded relationship between music and nature: the song of the nightingale which is pathetically invoked by Michael in his plea to relate to Julia.

This story is then a reworking of the Greek legend of Eurydice and Orpheus. In it, Eurydice dies of a snake bite on their wedding day. Orpheus, the greatest musician in the world, refuses to accept her death and descends to the underworld, where he sings so persuasively that Hades allows him to take back his bride, only to lose her again due to lingering doubt and weakness. *An Equal Music* reiterates this parable of love lost and almost regained by the power of music, the desperate bid to revive a dead romance against all odds, the subsequent anguish of heartbreak, and the agonies of accepting loss.

Vikram Seth's novel restores one's faith in the fictional form. It is a book written with a bone bleached economy of expression and emotion. As the novel progresses it implores the reader into a lucid silence. There is a sombre magic, a bracing, energizing after- glow that emanates from its pages. It places Seth in a tradition of modern fiction writers who have successfully combined a love story and the love of music as part of other narratives. His victory lies in his ability to create and sustain characters that have no direct relation to the author's cultural connection. There is a compelling lucidity and simplicity in his writing. In any work of art it is the variety which matters. Variety and the capacity to sustain variety are both a virtue and power. Seth shows both.

Quite poetic and moving are his words in the author's note to **An Equal Music** where Seth talks about three people in particular who helped him in giving as semblance of *An Equal Music* to his novel. They are a pianist, a percussionist and a string quartet player. He makes an interesting point, his heroine Julia is deaf yet she pursues the career of a musician. He interviewed a few doctors on deafness and in order to bring authenticity and synchronization of a deaf person's speech and lip movement, he attended lip reading classes for thirteen weeks. This shows that Seth never wanted to leave anything to chance. Whatever he contrived, he endeavored with full gusto and zeal.

Two types of stability, the first is, social and familial, and the other, mental and internal, are depicted in the novel. Also stressed again and again is the fact that attachment to love and music also leads to a sense of order and stability though of a different type, and **An Equal Music**, in spite of the individual's sense of loneliness, suggests that.

Vikram Seth's works reflect the sense of loss and dislocation he experienced as a migrant. Through the publication of his first collection of poetry, **Mappings**, Seth made his literary debut. Throughout the collection, Seth's Diasporic identity and its characteristics are highlighted. Numerous poems express the poet's themes of alienation, exile, rootlessness, loss, nostalgia, and other experiences. He has included his experiences with hybridity, multi-culturalism, and the search for identity into his writing because he is a migrant writer. The autobiographical components are very important in diasporas writing.

Seth's third book, ***An Equal Music (1999)***, has classical western music playing in the background and is set in London. Seth weaves together a love tale with a passion for music and a musician's way of life. The protagonist of the book is the musician Michael Holden, and the story revolves around his life. Society and culture are the two key areas that make up the socio-cultural idea. Community is a collection of individuals who belong to distinct societies, and culture is the way in which that community behaves as a whole. For example, performers, musicians, and singers from Europe migrate from one place to another extremely quickly. Vikram Seth illustrates his characters' cultures, traditions, and holidays.

Michael and Julia's terrible and lonely existence are explained by Seth, even though Michael wished to live with Julia. She wants to break the familiar link because she didn't like Nora in A Doll's House. Despite being a modern lady, Julia nevertheless observes conventions and abides by restrictions. The couple stayed within cultural bounds. Julia's married life has awoken her up to right behaviour. Michael's life was greatly impacted by the split. Although Michael and Julia are often bound in this circumstance, their culture would not permit them to act in a romantic manner.

Julia's deafness is an angle that evinces Seth's exploring the idea of a deaf musician-about being under the threat of losing music from a life that is dedicated to music. The character of Julia is based on famous deaf Evelyn Glennie, who Seth once dined with and was amazed to discover later she was deaf. He was then in the early stage writing *A Equal Music* and the idea of a deaf musician had its appeal. "Seth explains that after he had decided to bring Julia's deftness into the novel, he found a number of musicians who were quiet hard of hearing. Also, he interviewed doctors about deafness, so that the pacing of the onset of the disease was correct. He also took lip reading classes for thirteen weeks, in order to have a better understanding of how people who cannot cope with their ears cope through their eyes and in the case of musicians, also through the mind's ear." (16)

Unfolding Julia's deafness in a series of clues, Seth describes her as she tries to cope. Very well portrayed is the insensitivity of people towards deaf persons, in spite of their best intentions. Seth also reveals in a quiet manner the response of people upon learning of Julia's disability. Strangely enough, her fellow musicians are more accommodating of her deafness probably because they realize that when it comes to music there is a realm of mystery and a half-heard and half-imagined sound anyway. How could Beethoven have composed all those sonatas otherwise?

Seth does not seek to make Julia's deafness a metaphor to any other aspect of the novel. It is to be taken at face value; it is there, just as it is often there in real life. It is certainly more tragic since she is a musician, but resiliently, she allows her musical instincts to guide her back into proper musical functioning. Both Michael and Julia are very intense characters in large measures due to Seth's verbal dexterity that the novel accurately conveys a great deal of the emotion it inspires.

Among other noteworthy things in the novel is depiction of Michael's provincial boyhood at Rochdale in the north of England. The portrayal of a disadvantaged childhood north of England and industrialized landscape, the uprooting of human settlements the ill and aging father fixated on the family cat with the characteristic pathos-inducing loneliness of the very old, the gradual ebbing away of the life-blood of the town- all of it is skillfully delineated:

> "The handsome town hall presides over a waste--it is a town with its heart torn out. Everything speaks of its decline. Over the course of a century ……. it lost its work and its wealth. Then came the planning blight: the replacement of human slums by inhuman ones, the marooning of churches in traffic islands, the building of precincts where once there were shops. Finally, two

> decades of garroting from the
> government in London, and
> everything civic or social was
> choked of funds: schools,
> libraries, hospitals, transport.
> The town which had been the
> home of the Co-operative
> movement lost its sense of
> community." (17)

Also remarkable is Seth's marvelous sense of place, which entails in this instance the ability to conjure up visual spaces through aural cues. Seth has the knack for bringing a place to life by homing in on its uniqueness, and in this novel, this uniqueness is in what the place sounds like. The rising song of a lark evokes the moors of Rochdale; London is represented by songs of robins in winter and blackbirds in summer and by pigeons, Vienna is conjured up by the sound of nightingales, and Venice by the music of Vivaldi. Seth thus authenticates the novel by linking the profession of the characters with their sonic perception of the world.

As always with Seth, much of the pleasure that the novel provides is in its details and unhurried pace. The description on parks, long walks, the account of the water-serpents, London flat life, and the portrayal of the concierge at add to the texture rather than to its meaning. There are long description of Venice and Vienna, and few readers will grudge Seth that, owing to the excellence of his style, which in this novel is deeply evocative and emotional, yet sparse, highly appropriate when the characters are so intense. It comes as near to conveying the mercurial moods of love and of music as is possible in words.

London and Vienna are the locations used by Seth to illustrate British culture in *An Equal Music*. Seth makes no attempt to disparage the nation that previously colonized his homeland. Michael plays the second violin in the muggier quartet in this book. The plot of the book is on Michael's reaction to finding his long-lost love and his subsequent isolation. Michael and Julia first cross paths in Vienna, where they are both music students. Here, Seth paints a picture of two lovers who met while they were students and then reconciled after a long separation of ten years. They developed into important musicians in London and Vienna. Seth also depicts their struggles as classical musicians; including how rarely classical music is taught in English schools, how chamber music is waning in popularity, and how string quartets struggle to exist. The minute details of turnings of organizing a violin maker's performance and of the animosity discussions between the protagonists regarding intricacies of their performance show that Seth did much research before writing this book. The novels created by Seth have Diasporic characteristics.

In *An Equal Music*, Michael relocates from his rural birthplace to Vienna and later to the capital of London in order to pursue a musical career. Instead of adopting a pan-national identity, the character adopts a cosmopolitical identity. One of Diaspora's characteristics is this. Seth also relocates from one nation to another. He was born and raised in India, and while attending Nanjing University in China, Stan Ford in America, and Oxford in Britain, he travelled extensively. His creative output is a reflection of his in-depth familiarity with these various nations.

The fact that Michael is Batcher's son is ironic in itself, as revealed by *An Equal Music*, which shows Vikram Seth's love of irony. The story is better able to ground itself in the real world of man because to Seth's approaches to social reality. Michael plays the role of a social critic for his creator when he explains the changes in Rochdale. Michael and Julia's epic love story is told in this book by Seth, who has also built a live, breathing world that enchants and captivates the readers. Despite Julia being married to James, Seth showed discontinuous lovers who met after a long time and had a physical relationship. But neither Seth nor society find sexuality to be acceptable. The lifestyle of young people is portrayed by Vikram Seth as one of responsibility, dream, passion, love, suffering, and sacrifice. Seth is also interested in exploring western culture and classical music which evokes the nation's cultural prosperity and he successfully depicts the Diasporas elements in his novels like *An Equal Music* and *The Golden Gate.*

In *An Equal Music*, Seth takes a conventional romantic plot and renders it new and compelling through the attractive clarity and precision of its prose. One of the most impressive aspects of this novel is the way in which it manages to convey music through Michael's daily drama and battles as a member of a quartet. The reader is thrown into the lives, whims and chemistries of classical musicians. One would believe Seth himself has toured in a quartet to Venice and bid at auctions for violins. An incredible level of research has been undertaken, and Seth duly acknowledges the contributors. But Seth himself is modest about his musical abilities, yet the fact that he was commissioned to write a libretto (later published as *Arion and the Dolphin* (1994) for the English National Opera in 1994 suggests he is no novice. However in the book, there are several moments when intense discussions on Schubert, Schumann, and Bach become too tedious for us commoners.

4.(D) Plot of An Equal Music

The main plot, as the title indicates, concerns the quartet and their struggle with profession while the sub-plot centers on Michael's obsession with Julia, his estranged beloved whom he suddenly meets after a gap of ten years, and his Tononi that Mrs. Formby has lent him. Brief undercurrent of other issues are touched upon like Michael's ailing father revokes his connection with Michael's past, Rochdale that is slowly losing its natural charm; it also gets connected with the sub-plot, Tononi. Julia's husband and son are connected with the first sub-plot while Michael's lust for Virginie, the brief love relationship of Piers and Alex (Who was in place of Michael in the quartet) that discontinues due to the obvious homosexual angle, Michael's intense desire to give equal music to Julia by seeing her perform independently; all get connected with the main plot.

The sub-plot concerns Mrs. Formby and her contribution in Michael's life that eventually helps him in his profession. It becomes an important theme interwoven into the main plot. She is an old, childless widow and had initiated him into violin playing when he was barely nine years old. She willingly lent to him since she felt Michael deserved it. He feels it sings like his favorite bird, lark. He is afraid lest she gives it to someone else, for her nephew had a bigger claim on it and going by its increased value it was difficult for her to refuse him. Being a sensitive person she too was also reluctant to have it played by a stranger. Michael considers the issues with melancholy and passion. Howsoever strong his feelings may be, he is helpless and has to watch the situation with crossed fingers. Indeed, only a true artist likes Seth, who can feel the pulse of art, can transform such intense feelings into such beautiful, evocative and yet, simple words.

4.(E) Review of An Equal Music

The novel has a unique flavor - a strange pungent mingling of wild romance and domestic realism, of cosmic music and local details. Seth is not a belated romantic who hails from no school, nor has any successively writer produced a work of similar tang. The two chief characters are drawn with an unforgettable poetic intensity. *An Equal Music* links an exciting and romantic story to a sober and honest realism - a tragic story that ends with an Aristotelian catharsis for all the players in the drama.

The tone is poignant. Michael's discomfiture is conveyed which he reflects on the various instances shared by Julia and her family. His disturbed psyche while on one hand lures him to Julia; on the other hand, it makes him face the reality. He realizes that Julia's existence cannot be treated in isolation; she has to be conceived in totality, the woman who together with her husband and son has seen the hard times and the happy times. Disengaging and isolating her from her family would be a sin and Michael would not be happy, carrying the burden of a sinner. Such introspection can be treated as a viable answer to those supporting infidelity, extra-marital affairs.

David Davidar claims that unlike most writers of Indian origin, Seth is very honest about his work. He writes only what he believes in, instead of relying on time tested formulas. Seth has been lauded for "being honest enough to follow his inspiration and to opt for the universality and transcending power of the beauty of music". For example, Namita Gokhle argues that Vikram Seth "is international and should be appreciated as a writer about human beings, not as a peddler of Indian exotica ... Deeply rooted in his specific Indian identity, Vikram Seth is yet a citizen of the world in the best sense ... His genius should be evaluated in his control over his material, and in creating a credible world-in-itself which he can cohabit and explore."(18)

Vikram Seth portrays the lifestyle of the young people with their responsibility, dream, passion, love, pain, and sacrifice. This novel thus defines how the music and literature relate to the meaning and the concert of classical music in Europe in the late 20th century. It also illustrates the socio-economic status of London's entertainment specialists at the end of the 20th century. Seth is interested in exploring Western world classical music, which evokes the nation's cultural prosperity and he successfully depicts in the novel *An Equal Music.*

Seth's language of music can convey every minutes of the art form. The love story pales in comparison. Moving as Julia's meeting with Michael is (after the performance at Wigmore Hall), it cannot compare with the sublimity of the music that has preceded it, particularly of the arresting encore. Such is the kind of blending of description and emotion through which Seth strives to capture the inexpressible essence of music.

The characters in the novel are also totally immersed in their presence of long-dead composers, as corporeal as that of the musicians that perform their works: a world in which Michael's relationship with his Carlo Tononi violin is as real to him as his relationship with other members of the quartet or even with Julia.

Seth treats the performers lives as if they were extensions of the miseries and splendors experienced by the composers whose work they seek to express. Seth himself is as intensely involved with the music. Schubert is invoked several times in the novel, and Seth says of him, "His songs have such heavenly concision." (19)

This kind of empathy with music and musicians is significant because music is at the very heart of *An Equal Music*. Such is Seth's involvement with music. Commendably, most of the scenes and passages connected with music are convincing. Seth gets it consistently and impressively right. It is true that ***An Equal Music*** is substantially technical and can therefore be potentially distracting for every non-musically aware reader. In essence, music is what the novel chiefly addresses itself to and those who have been caught in the spell of music will note with widening eyes that Seth is able to call an extraordinary amount of that experience to the page. Thus the entire novel is enriched with the melody of music.

Vikram Seth had the privilege to be initiated into classical music in his formative days. His 'guru' Pandit Ammath was a disciple of Ustad Arnir Khan, the great Maestro of Hindustani Classical Music. Later he had the opportunity to delve deep into the intricacies of Western Classical music and his emotional attachment to the world of music increased to its farthest limit. ***An Equal Music*** displays, in the true sense, a world of music, where the characters, mostly musicians, are found humming the tune or the 'half-tuneless tune' of one of the masters like Schubert, Mozart, Haydn, Brahms, Bach and Beethoven. The bliss of this world is suggested in the lines from John Donne quoted as an epigraph at the beginning of the novel. The strong power of Donne's imagination, coupled with this serene state blessed with 'equal light", 'equal music and equal eternity. The choice of these lines as the motto of the novel reveals Vikram Seth's psychological insight as well.

The conclusion of the novel is even-handed and utterly believable, with Michael holding on, not to Julia, but to a shared memory. When he hears Julia playing, to him "it is a beauty beyond imagining-clear, lovely. Inexorable, phrase is across phrase, phrase echoing phrase, the incomplete, the unending Art of Fugue. It is an equal music." (20) (*An Equal Music p-380*). The philosophy of aestheticism inherent in these closing lines marks a moment of epiphany for him, making him realize that "Music, such music is a sufficient gift. Why ask for happiness; why hope not to grieve: it is enough, it is to be blessed enough, to live from day to day and hear such music-not too much, or the soul could not sustain it -from time to time". (21) At the heart of this epiphany stands Bach's great fugue. In Spanish the word *fuga* means a "musical composition in counterpoint, based on the use of imitation of a short, but well differentiated theme," (22) (El Pequeno

Larousse Ilustrado, 469, 1996 ed.) and the *punto de fuga* is the point in a drawing done in perspective where straight parallel lines converge. The ending of the novel thus becomes the punto de fuga, "the point at which in art, straight parallel lines converge, due to perspective." (23) This is because at the end of the novel, Michael is alone like he was in the beginning, but there is one important difference: his thoughts have reached a resolution and he is no longer troubled. He has learned acceptance and it has brought him serenity. This change in perspective has enabled him to come to terms with his past made the present bearable, and the future promising. And perhaps most essentially of all, he has realized that to be complete is an advantage not a necessity.

The novel thus reiterates Seth's earlier philosophy of value of such mundane institutions as home and family. It is story about the ultimate triumph of sanity over human irrationality, and a seeking to create a balance between personal and artistic worlds. It explores loneliness, especially the loneliness of an artist, and seeks to portray the interface of creativity with the unavoidable tensions of daily life. It is also about the joy of having regained what was thought to be lost forever, coupled with the anguish of realization and denial, It is impassioned and poetic, elegiac and witty by turns, and set against the Augustan backdrop of Venice and Vienna, it is a fit stage tor the unfurling of a love tale to the music of Beethoven and Bach. Seth's obvious passion for his subject and his subsequent empathy with it lend this novel an extra dimension. This, together with his talent for words and imagery and an excellent literary ending make this novel an exceptional read.

Refrences :-

1. Seth Vikram, <u>An Equal Music</u>, New Delhi: Viking Penguin Book, 1999. India (P) Ltd.p-16
2. An Equal Music p-306
3. An Equal Music p-165
4. Sara Crowe, "No ice, Vikram," A Talk at the Seymour Centre, The University of Sidney News, March 23, 2000
5. Gupta Roopali, Vikram Seth's Art: An Appraisal, New Delhi: Atlantic Publishers and Distributors Ltd. p-79-80
6. Vidyasagar, N. "In the Business of Books" Interview with Vikram Seth. The Times of India 11 April 1999
7. Seth, Vikram. "An Equal Music." Penguin Books, 2000. p-47
8. Seth, Vikram. "An Equal Music." Penguin Books, 2000.p-242-243
9. Seth, Vikram. "An Equal Music." Penguin Books, 2000.p- 253-254
10. Carey, John. "Music for the Mind". Review. The Sunday Times 28 Mar. 1999.
11. Seth Vikram, <u>An Equal Music</u>, New Delhi: Viking Penguin Book, 1999. India (P) Ltd.p-15
12. An Equal Music p-69
13. An Equal Music p-5
14. An Equal Music p-20
15. Helperin John, ed., <u>The Theory of Novel</u> (London: Oxford University Press, 1974. P-64

16. Ruth Alexander and Isabella Perriera, "Dark Lord of the Seth," Cherwell-The Independent Oxford University Newspaper. URL:www.planet-hardcore-/Cherwell/archive/ht00/3/features/6.html

17. An Equal Music p-71

18. Gokhale, Namita. "Vikram's Vocalist Strains on Literary Landscape." Delhi; The Times ofIndia 4 May 1999; p-4

19. Sarah Bryan, "Author Seth Rhapsodizes on a String Quartet", St. Louis Post Dispatch, June. 10, 1999.

20. An Equal Music p-380

21. An Equal Music p-381

22. El Pequeno Larousse Ihustrado, 469, 1996 ed.

23. Fausta, URL:www.barnesandnoble.com/bookshelf/fictionbest1.asp

Conclusion

Vikram Seth's novels are notable for their stylistic experimentation and mercurial shifts in tone. With **The Golden Gate** he instantly established himself as quite possibly, the most formally inventive and technically adventurous of Asian American Writers. Yet, many of its stylistic characteristics and major themes stem from the same impulses that have given rise to his other major works. The most striking feature of *The Golden Gate* is its revival of the trimetric sonnet from of Alexander Pushkin's verse novel Eugene Onegin. His next novel *A Suitable Boy* has the distinction of being one of the longest novels in English literature. Seth has stated that it has taken him about a decade to complete the writing of the novel. And it is followed by the novel *An Equal Music* which deals with western music at great length in addition to the story revolving around the protagonist in whose first person narrative the novel is structured.

Seth's subject matter is almost invariably love, in all its myriad manifestations. He does explore other themes in passing, India's political landscape for instance or religions frenzy, but in these instances his role is always that of a storyteller, not of a commentator. He does feel strongly about issues like religious intolerance, nuclear non-proliferation, but he is not a social activist. Consequently, there is no social gravitas in his writing. He feels that the characters should ring true to the people's lives they portray Seth's characters are thus chiefly involved in getting on with their lives and as an artist Seth's primary concern is to portray them indulging in activities that are in a general sense, common to all humanity. Seth also places great emphasis on the redeeming aspects of private life, portraying in his work that happiness and tolerance start from home. The unifying theme that runs through his work are the plea for human camaraderie, spanning political, national and cultural barriers. Seth's writing is an embodiment of his intrinsic tolerance, a tolerance that is remarkably Chaucer-like, extending itself to include all the foibles of human behavior and evident specially in his acute distress at the destruction of humanity by humans.

Seth is firm about his priorities as an artist he places intelligibility above verbal pyrotechnics. Also, he tends towards realism in all his work. This is evident in Seth's re-creation of worlds which always ring true, whether he is writing a story about west coast America, India of the 1950s or the world of Schubert and Mozart. However, Seth believes, like Goethe that the artist's work is real in so far as it is always true: ideal in that it is never actual. Seth is an accomplished artist and treads with considerable poise this fine line, rendering the near and the familiar with artistic verisimilitude.

Seth presents love in its all shades and in all dimensions whether it is *A Suitable Bov*, *An Equal Music, or The Golden Gate* Inter-religious love is seen at the very outset in **A Suitable Boy**: Kabir Durani, a Muslim boy is in love with Lata Mehra, a Hindu girl; love between high status and low status i.e. Maan, a man who belongs to an aristocratic family and Saeeda Bai, a woman with low status and character, a courtesan; one sided love of tutor Rasheed for his student Tasneem; Firoz and Imitiaz admiring the Teenager Tasneem; apart from

Kabir there are two more admirers of Lata: Amit, a poet and Haresh Khanna, a shoe maker; illicit love relation is seen between Mr. Billi Irani and Meenakshi Chatterjee which comes under the category of extra- marital affair, snort glimpses of the presence of Haresh Khanna and Simran, Kakoli and Hans represent the love for each other. Love among the friends is governed by Malati (best friend if Lata, always ready to help her in need); friendship between Maan and Firoz exists just because of love between them, among the true friends also comes the name of Mahesh Kapoor and Nawab Sahib whose friendship remained stable in all the conditions. Mother-daughter love between Mrs. Mehra and her daughter Lata gives strength to their relationship and ultimately for her mother's sake Lata drops up Kabir and chooses Haresh Khanna as her life-mate. It is the father's love that makes Mahesh Kapoor worried about his killer son Maan and wants to take him out of the prison. Mahesh Kapoor, Anun Mehra and Haresh Khanna are the individuals who are overpowered with the love of nations, profession and principles: the first is a patriotic man and loves his own country; the second one has respect for the

Western country; and the latter is the one who has respect and love for both the countries. The similarity between them is that all of them have love for their profession and rely on specific principles. Uncle Shanti is another character who is devoted to his profession, he loves his work of dentistry, and he continues his work for a long time though it was performed with his left arm. Love for power enlivens all the politicians to win and usurp the election whether it is Mahesh Kapoor or L. N. Agarwal. Love of pets is in the form of cuddles in the Chatterji family When we turn towards *An Equal Music.* Michael Holme is deeply in love with a fellow student, Julia McNicoll; love for the music of Beethoven and Bach; each and every member of the Maggiore Quartet has deep love for their instruments especially Michael's attachment to his violin-Carlo-Tononi. Music paves path for the spirituality and the one who is nearer to music is considered near to soul and lastly finds its destination. It is the love for music that reunites Michael and Julia for some time, it has a spiritual charm that cannot be resisted and finally the musicians accomplished their target of playing the Maggiore Quartet. The significance of love in one's life is very abruptly understood in the writings of Vikram Seth.

Seth depicts very well the estrangement, frustration, materialism and alienation of modern man in western society: Michael leads a life of isolation after his departure from Vienna, in **The Golden Gate,** John Brown, the hero, a Silicon valley computer professional is seen in continuous hunt for love, is estranged and feels isolated among the individual's of his group, Janet Hayakawa on the other hand is frustrated who has a secret desire for John but, she is not enough courageous to express her feelings to him. In *A Suitable Boy* Arun Mehra and Meenakshi Chatterji represent the modern man turning towards the western culture whose living style is influenced by the western culture and both are materialistic in attitudes. Seth makes it clear that there are people who are unable to flare up their sentiments, sometimes love makes a man to suffer and sometimes it is reached to fullest.

Another prevailing theme is marriage. In *A Suitable Boy*, the novel begins with the marriage of Savita and Pran kapoor, and ends with the wedding of Lata and Haresh Khanna. More emphasis is laid on the arranged marriages: all the four major families are a result of arranged marriages where husbands are considered as equivalent to God as is in case of Mrs. Kapoor, who worships her husband and never tries to object on to wrong decisions; re-marriage betwcen Dr. Kishan Chand Seth and Parvati: the Abdhur Rasheed's marriage to his elder brother's widow; then Arun Mehra of Brahmpur is married to Meenakshi Chatterji of West Bengal representing the inter-state marriages. Seth has presented the reality of people and had tried to show the mirror of society. In *An Equal Music*, marriage is a necessity for young girls to protect themselves from the thorn of society: Julia's marriage proved a successful one as Hansen was always with her in the hours of need, he gave full support when Julia was going deaf and suggested her to attend the lip reading classes, supported her to gain her ambition of playing for the Maggiore Quartet. It is marriage which serves as a protection from the evil threat of society.

Family is a prominent theme in Seth's works: in *A Suitable Boy* Seth introduces the four kinds of families which peep in the existence joint family; an individual feels supportive in such family; Lata and Maan's decision signifies this truth that family serves as a safeguard members. The interest of modem man is diverting towards the single family as 1hey find no charm in a joint family rather consider it as a burden to live the relation, everyone wants the freedom to take the independent decisions which are prohibited in such families as the whole family has to obey the head of the family. *A Suitable Boy* deals with the post-Independence India where the joint family was the most commanding one. In ***An Equal Music*** the characters survive in an individual environment, the family introduced is secluded: Michael is seen with his mother and father who is a butcher by profession; Julia with her husband and son makes the family. Western culture believes in separate family where joint family has no charm.

Seth focuses on the certainty and presence of nature, as it plays a very crucial role in presenting the accurate thoughts and sentiments of the characters. In ***A Suitable Boy,*** Lata is seen sitting under the Gulmohar tree after her exam; she takes pleasure of nature by riding with Kabir on a boat on the banks of Ganga; while reading the poems she hear the sweet voice of the nightingales and so on. Similarly, *An Equal Music* has also a nature touch in it as it has been conceived in the garb of nature. Michael's visits to Hyde Park, morning swims in filthy, freezing water of Serpentine, the rain, the garden of Julia, the melodious songs of larks and nightingales, the mention of lilacs in bloom and many such descriptions signify the veracity of the nature throughout the novel. Seth is conspicuous while involving nature in his writings. In *The Golden Gate* nature receives a due share of attention in each blossoming shrub, each swathe of colour in nature's autumn finery, the slow march of seasons, the biannual migration of the birds and whales and many more. Seth describes the natural beauty of the Bay Area, as opposed to the artificiality of life controlled by technology.

Society is something which is formed by the combination of culture, religion and principles to be obeyed. Seth is not untouched by its vitality and it is proved in his writings where society acts as a leading part in an individual's life and decisions. In *A Suitable Boy*, it is the society which is a stumbling block in the path of beloveds; it is the society which resists an inter-religious love or marriage; a love between a noble man and a prostitute or illicit relations illustrating the utmost power of the society. If society favors crooked works, there could have been no peace and humanism. The fear of society stops a man from doing an evil as. Seth acknowledges that society serves as a safeguard for the human beings and enables them to live a healthy and happy life. It is society that makes Maan and Lata to be practical in taking correct decisions of leaving Seedaa Bai and Kabir. Seth has made it clear that a society has its own customs and beliefs whether it is an Indian society or American society in *The Golden Gate.*

Many families together constitute a society and society is governed by religion. Each and every character is influenced by the religion. In *A Suitable Boy*, Seth draws the portrait of religion and its effect on the individual characters; there are rules and regulations which must be followed by the people belonging to the particular religion. Religion is something which forbids a person to cross its limitations as Kabir and Lata are restricted to continue their relationship further for the sake of religion. Muslims pray in Maszids and Hindus in temples, religion teaches humanism, peace and prosperity but people in the name of religion are ever prepared to take off he lives mercilessly. The episode of Shiva Lingam on the disputed site, the Raja of Marh lays the foundation stone of the temple, the Imam of the Alamgiri Mosque gives an inflammatory speech on Friday Moharram and Dussera, the holy speeches near the bunks of the Ganga pinpoints towards the greatness of religion as involvement in these rituals gives people solace and peace of mind. In *The Golden Gate* it was the Catholic upbringing that taught Ed the religiosity of nature and he decided to live a decent relationship. Homosexuality is the burning theme which is seen in the characters of Seth as In *A Suitable Boy* Maan and Firoz are accompanied by the homosexual relationship, in *An Equal Music*, Piers, one of the player of music in the Maggoire Quartet represents this kind of relationship; in **The Golden Gate**, Liz's (Elizabeth Dorati) brother

Ed (Fdward Dorati') has secret ties with Phil. Seth has extracted the hidden facets of life in front of the readers and had tried to make aware of the fast passage of time.

Exploitation has its own specific criteria in Seth's writings. When a person is asked to perform a task which is against his ego, principles or is tortured mentally or physically it signifies that he is being exploited. In *A Suitable Boy*, exploitation is done by the people in the name of Hindu and Muslims and Zamindars are ever ready to exploit their tenants. Seth mirrors up that the exploitation in the name of religion must be readily avoided as God is one and he never wishes death and destruction to prevail on the earth. Thus, these are the major themes which frequently existed through his novels but still there are inumerable minor themes preserved in its garb. In *A Suitable Boy*, the Zamindari Abolition has created threat among the Zamindars as is with the Rasheed's father who is a Zamindar, Colonisation exists in the novel through Arun Mehra and his wife Mcenakshi Chatterjee as they have transformed themselves in the western culture and always boast of the British Culture. Since *A Suitable Boy* is written on the post-independent India and as it is a democratic country it cannot be kept aloof from the politics. Seth summarizes that without education life is vacant and meaningless. It is education where one gets acquainted with friendly and refined manners and adds nobility to the character and ultimately one develops a perfect personality which is the main point of attraction to all In *The Golden Gate* Seth has portrayed the intimate Californian lifestyles, house-warming parties' weekend and almost all the facets of life. Nuclear Warfare has its own existence and Seth picks up the underpinning issues of it from the mouth of Phil, who shows his revolt against the Space and Missile race.

All the three above mentioned novels are abundant in portraying the regional descriptions In *A Suitable Boy*, the beauty of Brahmpur is revealed; in *An Equal Music*, the Silicon Valley draws the attention of the readers. Seth uses chapterisation technique in his entire novel: *A Suitable Boy*, consists of nineteen parts, overall each part is divided into twenty one sub-parts; *An Equal Music*, consists of eight parts; and ***The Golden Gate***, carries in itself thirteen parts. This division gives the novel a systematic and attractive outlook: it makes the reader understand the novel and maintains the interest; every part helps in the movement of the plot, from the beginning to the middle, then to climax and bid a suitable end. Thus, it will be no exaggeration to say that Vikram Seth is a name enriched with all the prose and poetic qualities which possess an overpowering charm and a majestic power.

Occasionally, Seth can be seen substituting one part of speech for another, what Corbett and Connors call anthimeria. The novelist has used noun as verb and vice-versa. This stylistic feature has also been exploited by the greater writers like Shake speare and Milton. Thus, Seth can be compared with the great writers of the world in terms of artistic expression. It is to be noted that the coinages by Seth are basically drawn from English lexicon but they are semantically new ones. Obviously, Seth did not create new words to enrich the lexical resources of English; rather he coined them for the purpose of highlighting the delicacies of particular contexts of the novels. It is also to be noted that Seth is not only interested in the verbal painting but also in the subtle portrait of the evanescent emotions of his characters. He employs modal auxiliaries to present different psychic states of his characters. Through them the novelist has shown the world-views of his men and women. (1) (*Sonba M. Salve, The Novels of Vikram Seth: A Thematic and Stylistic Study, Prestige Books International, New Delhi. p-160*)

Seth's poetic style finds its manifestation successfully through the phonological devices like alliteration, assonance, onomatopoeia, rhyme and rhythm. Seth loves different music in different things and can be seen expressing the nuances of the theme with the help of beautiful sound effects. The phonological patterns highlight the utterances and render them musical. They also add to the effect of the expression and impart it poetic air and coloring in the case of prose. One can say that Seth by using right sounds is able to evoke the required mood and atmosphere for his universe. Thus, the novelist has exploited phonological devices as rhetorical or stylistic devices for the purpose of persuasion. Similarly, the figures like simile, metaphor, personification, apostrophe, hyperbole, rhetorical question, question tag, synecdoche have been employed as semantic devices in the novels. These figures enable the novelist to express the powerful feelings of the characters. We have observed that these figures add emotional intensity to the informative statements and say much about the theme in a little space. Therefore, they are the brighter spots of Seth's style and theme. (2) (*Sonba M. Salve, The Novels of Vikram Seth: A Thematic and Stylistic Study, Prestige Books International, New Delhi. p-161)*

Seth advocates the values like affection, mutual consideration and compatibility that make sure ground for the success of any relationship, be it marriage or family or friendship. He regards marriage and family as essential means of educating and improving the men and women. He suggests that the meaning of life is to be found in the renunciation of passion and tolerant participation in the comic parliament of marriage, family and togetherness.

Thus, Vikram Seth is a serious writer whose broad vision contributes to the idea of safety and solidarity of the entire society. Seth's vision is not the newest or extraordinary but the way or the style through which he presents it is extraordinary. To quote Graham Hough, "the important truths are all known in advance and that the function of the writer is chiefly to present the familiar in a striking and effective manner." (2) (*Graham Hough, The Mind of Europe, Style and Stylistics (London Routledge and Kegan Paul, 1969), p-48.*)

Seth's deviation in the use of language in his novels certainly helps in the establishment of a new trend in the Indian writing in English. Though the dramas and the novels have been written in verse by earlier writers like Shakespeare, T.S. Eliot and others; but in modern generation, Seth's versification of his novels is a unique experiment in the world of literature, particularly in the history of Indian English literature. For these reasons, Seth certainly stands out among the Indian English writers. It is quite appropriate to say that due to the dazzling versatility of theme and style, Seth is the poet, the translator, the travel writer, the librettist and above all the novelist of a different order.

Furthermore, since Seth's works show the marked linguistic consciousness, his novels deserve a fruitful enquiry from the, stylistic point of view Perhaps it is for this reason, G.J.V. Prasad observes "Vikram Seth, the poet and the novelist is so much in control of language that he does not care about the content as much as he does about the form or style." (3) (*G.J.V. Prasad, "The Solitary Wanderer -The Seth of the Garden, Vikram Seth: An Anthology of Recent Criticism (Delhi, Pen craft international, 2004), p-33.*) Indeed, Seth takes meticulous care of his style which is highly poetic, unique, original and amply communicative. Seth's style is one of the major factors of his exemplary success as writer who has made his mark on the international audience.

Refrences :-

1. Sonba M. Salve, The Novels of Vikram Seth: A Thematic and Stylistic Study, Prestige Books International, New Delhi. p-160

2. Sonba M. Salve, The Novels of Vikram Seth: A Thematic and Stylistic Study, Prestige Books International, New Delhi. p-161

3. Graham Hough, The Mind of Europe, Style and Stylistics (London Routledge and Kegan Paul, 1969), p. 48.

4. G.J.V. Prasad, "The Solitary Wanderer -The Seth of the Garden, Vikram Seth: An Anthology of Recent Criticism (Delhi, Pen craft international, 2004), p-33

5. Seth Vikram, The Golden Gate, (New Delhi): Penguin (p) Ltd

6. Roopali Gupta, Vikram Seth's Art: An Approsal, Atlantic Publishers and Distributors Ltd

7. Seth Vikram, "A Suitable Boy" Viking Penguin Ltd. 1993.

8. Seth, Vikram. "An Equal Music." Penguin Books, 2000.

Bibliography

Primary Sources

Novels

<u>The Golden Gate</u>: A Novel in Verse. London: Faber, 1986; New Delhi: Oxford University Press, 1986.

<u>A Suitable Boy</u>, New Delhi: Penguin, 1993.

<u>An Equal Music</u>, New Delhi: Penguin Books India (P) Ltd. 1999.

Non- Fiction

<u>Two Lives</u>, New Delhi: Viking, 2005.

Travelogue

<u>From Heaven Lake</u>: Travels Through Sinkiang and Tibet.

London: Hogarth Press, 1983; New Delhi: Penguin, 1990.

Translation

Three Chinese Poets: Translations of Poems by Wang Wei,

Li Bai and Du Fu,

London: Faber, 1992.

Libretto

Arion and the Dolphin, London: Phoenix, 1994.

Poetry

Mappings, Calcutta: Writers Workshop, 1981; New Delhi:

Penguin, 1994.

The Humble Administrator's Garden, Manchester

and New York: Carcanet, 1985;

New Delhi: Oxford University Press, 1987.

All You who Sleep Tonight, London: Faber, 1990;

New Delhi: Penguin, 1990.

Beastly Tales From Here and There, London: Phoenix, 1993.

The Collected Poems, New Delhi: Penguin, 1995.

Secondary Sources

Agaruallah, Shyam S. Vikram Seth's *A suitable Boy*: *search for an Indian identify*. New Delhi: prestige, 1995.

Agarwallah, Shyam S. Vikram Seth's *A suitable Boy: Search for an Indian Identify* New Delhi: Prestige, 1995.

Alam, Fakrul. *South Asian Writers in English Tomson Gale*, 2006.

Alam, Fakrul. *South Asian Writers in English.* MI: Thomson Gale, 2006. xxiii, 490.

Alexander, Meena. "Vikram seth," post colonial studies at Emory. 9 Mar 2003.   Anand, Mulk Raj. Preface, *Two leaves and A bud*. Delhi orient Paperbacks: 1969. Anand, Mulkraj *Apology for Heroism Bombay*: Kutub Popular: 1957.

Anand, Mulkraj Preface, Two Leaver and a Bud Delhi orient paperbacks: 1969. Anand, Mulkraj. *Apology for Heroism*, Bombay: Kutub Popular, 1957.

C. Vijaysree, *"Vikram Seth"*, *Writers of The Indian Diaspora*, ed, Emmanual s. Nelson, Greenwood Press, CT, 1993

Chakravarth, Joya. *Indian Writing in English: Perspective*. New Delhi: Atlantic Publishers and Distributors, 2003. Xi, 161.

Dhawan, R.K. *50 years of Indian Writing : Golden Jubilee* Volume, New Delhi: Indian Association for English Studies, [1999] . 160.

Gopal, N.R. and Suman Sachar *Indian English Poetry and Fiction: A Critical Evaluation.* New Delhi: Atlantic Publishers and DIstributors, 2000. xxii, 238.

Gupta, Roopali. *Vikram Seth's Art: An Appraisal.*New Delhi: Altantic Publishers & Distributors, 2005. vii, 136.

Gupta, Santosh. *The Golden gate: The First Indian Novel in Verse.* The New Indian Novel in English: A study of the 1980s. Viney Kirpal (Ed). New Delhi: Allied Publishers Ltd., 1990.91-100.

Guravi Gujrat, "*The Astouding Success of Vikram Seth*", Unsigned, 3 April 1993.

Iyengar, K.R. Srinivasa *Indian writing in English Bombay* Asia Pub House, 1973.

Jeremy Gavron, "*A Suitable Boy*" Daily Mail and Gaurdian, July, 20, 1999.

Jha, Ashok K. Vikram Seth: *The Golden Gate and Other Writings Recent Indian Fiction*. R.S. Pathak (Ed), New Delhi: Prestige books, 1994. 54- 70.

Karunakaran, Supriyaa. *Gamesh the Novelists Play: The subsversive Rebellion of Vikram Seth in The Golden Gate and Shashi Tharoor's THe Great Indian Novel, Fiction of Nineties*. Veena Noble and R.K. Dhawan Dass (Eds.) New Delhi: Prestige Books, 1994.93-97.

Kumar, Sathish *A survey of Indian of Indian English novel: Bareilly*; Prakesh Book Depot, 1996. Kumar, Satish. *A Survey of Indian English Novel Bareilly*: Prakash Book depot; 2006.

Kumar, V.L.V.N. Narendra *New perspectives on Indian Writing*. New Delhi: prestige Books, 1997.135.

M.K.Naik. *A History of Indian English Literature*, New Delhi: Sahitya Akademi, 1982

Makarand Paranjape, *"A Conversation with Vikram Seth, Mixed Beats and Cultural Products"*, Indian Review of books (2)6, 1993

Mohanty, Seemita *A critical Analysis of Vikram Seth's Poetry and fiction* New Delhi Atlantic, 2007.

Myers, David. *Vikram Seth's Epic Renunciation of the Passions: Deconstructing Moral Codes in A Suitable Boy, Fiction of the Nineties*. Veena Noble and R. K. Dhawan Dass(Eds.) New Delhi: Prestige Books, 1994. 719)

Myers, David. *Vikram Seth's Epic Renunciation of the Passions: Deconstructing Moral Codes in A Suitable Boy, Indian Literature Today*: Vol. I: Drama and Fiction. R. K. Dhawan(Ed.) New Delhi: Prestige Books, 1994. 79-10)

Naiker, Basavaraj. *Indian English Literature*: Vol.IV New Delhi: Atlantic Publishers & Distributors, 2003, xi, 324.

Narayen, Leela Lakshmi. *The Golden Bridge is Falling Down, Falling Down, Falling Down: A Study of Vikram Seth's The Golden Gate*, Critical Responses: Commonwealth Literature. . New Delhi: Sterling Publihsers Pvt. Ltd., 1993, 174-183.

Nona Walia, Interview, *"in the Humble Authors's Garden"*, Times Life! Times of India, Nov, 20, 2005

Patil, Z.N. *The Image of America in Vikram Seth's The Golden Gate, Commonwealth Writing*: A Study in Expatriate Experience. R. K. and L. S. R.

Krishna Sastry Dhawan New Delhi: Prestige Books, 1994. 21-29.

Pawan K. Verma, " *Of love, Loneliness and the Fine Art of storytelling*" Hindustan times (Delhi) Sunday magazine May, 2, 1999.

Pramod K. Nayar's and R.K. Dhavan's *Vikram Seth, the Literary Genius: An Introduction,*prestge books, 2005

Prasad, Amar Nath and S. John Peter Joseph *Indian Writing in English* : Critical Ruminations: Vol.2 New Delhi: Sarup and Sons, 2006. xi, 283.

Prasad, G.J.V., Vikram Seth: *An Anthology of Recent Criticism* , Delhi: Pencraft International, 2004.191.

Ramaswamy, S. A Sonata in C Major: *Viam Seth's The Golden Gate, Essays in Criticism on Indian Literature in English.* M. S., N. Eakambaram and A. Natarajan Nagarajan (Jt. Eds.) New Delhi: S. Chand & Company, 1991. 152-161. Ramaswamy, S. *A Sonata in Major Viam Seth's The Golden Gate*, Commentaries on Commonwealth Fiction. S. Ramaswamy. New Delhi: Prestige Books, 1994. 189-201

Richard B. Woodward, *Vikram Seth's Big Book*", New York Times, May, 2 1993

Salman Rushdie, the Ground Beneath Her Feet Newyork: Henry Holt and Company 1999.

Shyamala A. Narayan, "A Suitable Boy: An Exemplar of Artististic Freedom, The Quest, Vol. 8, No. 2, December 1994

Singh, A. K. *Vikram Seth's A Suitable Boy: A Critique, Indian Fiction of the - Nineties*. R. S. Pathak (Ed.) New Delhi: Creative Books, 1997, 11-28.

Sonba M. Salve, *The Novels of Vikram Seth: A Thematic and Stylistic Study*, Prestige Books International, New Delhi. 2009

Vikram Seth, "writers on writing" Radio Series Transcript. Australian Broadcasting Corporation URL: http://www.abe.net.au/writers/writers summary

Internet Sources

Fausta,

URL:www.barnesandnoble.com/bookshelf/ficti onbest1.asp

https://coolienovel.blogspot.com/2022/01/theme s-of-coolie-coolie-is-great-work.html

https: // en.m.wikipedia.org.

https://www.gradesaver.com/swami-and-friends/study-guide/themes

https://www.gentlemengyan.com/2022/07/theme s-issues-in-novel-untouchable-m-r.html

https://www.litcharts.com/lit/swami-and-friends.

https://quizsansar.in/define-r-k-narayan-as-a-novelist

https://www.shareyouressays.com/knowledge/essay-on-the-r-k-narayans-writing-style-and-languages/118120

https://www.shareyouressays.com/knowledge/salient-features-of-r-k-narayans-prose-style-in-the-bachelor-of-arts/118091

https://smartenglishnotes.com

https://www.the-criterion.com

Rediff.coom Interview URL

www.rediff.com/chat/vikcha.html